PATHWAY TO A PENSION

Jack Sutherland

PATHWAY TO A PENSION

iUniverse books may be ordered through booksellers or by contacting:

iUniverse
1663 Liberty Drive
Bloomington, IN 47403
www.iuniverse.com
844-349-9409

ISBN: 978-1-6632-1757-8 (sc)
ISBN: 978-1-6632-1758-5 (e)

Library of Congress Control Number: 2021901702

Print information available on the last page.

iUniverse rev. date: 01/26/2021

Dedicated to
Coline, my wife, and our three adult children,
Jennifer, Sara, and Mark.

ABOUT THE AUTHOR

Jack Sutherland is a retired community banker with a 40+ year career helping small businesses and their owner families achieve their business and personal financial goals. He has been a financial services industry thought leader, offering his insights on business topics based on his personal and professional experience. He is also a Vietnam veteran, an entrepreneur, and a self-published author.

Sutherland, a Missouri native, graduated from the University of Missouri-Columbia with both a bachelor of science (BS) and a master of business administration (MBA) degree. He was awarded the Certificate of Merit in 2011 for his professional achievements in banking and his service to the university's Trulaske College of Business.

He is also the founder and managing partner of a private alternative investment fund. He currently is active on two for-profit boards of directors.

Sutherland has extensive business experience and enjoys writing on the subjects he is most enthusiastic about, offering guidance to others who want to help themselves. If you want to improve your financial life, he is willing to work with you. His books deal with topics like saving and investing for retirement, creating a grand strategy for survival for small towns, and the vital importance of sharing financial information between spouses. His latest publication outlines a pathway to achieving a lifetime retirement paycheck.

Books by Jack Sutherland:

- *PUT TIME ON YOUR SIDE*
  How to Achieve Financial Independence in Retirement

- *TIME TO CATCH UP*
  Powerful Strategies to Accelerate Retirement Funding

- *INVESTING 1.0.1 WITH PURPOSE*
  Taking the Mystery Out of Investing

- *SMALL TOWNS STILL MATTER*
  A Grand Strategy for Survival

- *BEFORE I GO . . .*
  Sharing Is Caring: The Vital Importance of Sharing Financial Information between Spouses

- *PATHWAY TO A PENSION*
  Follow My Rules of Engagement to a Lifetime Retirement Paycheck

The author and his wife reside in Overland Park, Kansas. They enjoy their retirement and time with their three adult children and four grandchildren.

CONTENTS

PART ONE

FRAMEWORK OF A RETIREMENT CRISIS

PART TWO

MY RULES OF ENGAGEMENT: SEVEN WINNING FINANCIAL STRATEGIES

PART THREE

ENJOY YOUR PENSION

PART ONE

FRAMEWORK OF A RETIREMENT CRISIS

INTRODUCTION

"Retirement security is often compared to a three-legged stool supported by Social Security, employer-provided pension funds, and private savings."

– Sander Levin –

America has a looming retirement crisis, and it is getting worse! The gap between actual savings and the projected amount needed for a secure retirement nest egg is becoming a deep fault line, leading to serious financial concerns for those retiring over the next few decades.

Too many people believe their Social Security benefits will cover more than they actually do, and too many people have little or no savings. This pending crisis is growing even worse because they are not doing enough to change their financial behavior.

This is the current landscape of retirement planning. Retirement prospects seem grim for over half of Americans, according to the latest results from a GOBankingRates survey. The survey revealed that more people would retire broke than originally projected.

The GOBankingRates survey found that 64% of Americans are expected to retire with less than $10,000 in their retirement accounts. Why are Americans delaying or ignoring saving for retirement?

Among many reasons cited, five of the most frequent ones were:

1. "I don't make enough money to save."
2. "I am struggling just to pay my bills."
3. "My priority is paying down debt, not saving."
4. "The coronavirus pandemic has frozen all my future financial decision-making. Who can plan with such a high level of uncertainty?"
5. "I live for today. Tomorrow may never come."

These are not legitimate reasons for avoiding funding a retirement account. They are *excuses*, because they prolong an individual's procrastination on retirement planning—the default behavior of far too many people. Removing your self-imposed limitations and moving beyond complacency can allow you to overcome your excuses. Ultimately, excuses prevent growth and create regret, causing you to look back and say, "I wish I would have . . ."

These are not ordinary times. The strongest force in human nature, fear, should be driving a change. But it is not! In reality, too many Americans just don't care enough about saving for retirement. Ultimately, this group may have no other option than working past their full retirement age or never retiring. They are hoping the federal government will solve their retirement dilemma. They want universal access to retirement savings plans, mandatory employer-sponsored plans, and automatic enrollment in these plans. In essence, they want the government to compel them into a retirement plan. They want an employer-sponsored pension plan.

Hope is not a strategy! When you enter retirement, a financial do-over is not permitted. It is too late to make up for the years of neglect and underfunding for retirement. *PATHWAY TO A PENSION* offers some practical guidance for many of the most crucial financial decisions you will need to make before you enter retirement. After all, retirement is not a specific age; it's more about achieving a financial number to give you the option of retiring.

According to Andy Smith, host of the call-in radio program *Investing Sense*, "People are just not saving enough. You need to save as much as you can for as long as you can. We live in a one-size-fits-nobody world and the average American is time-bankrupt, as retirement costs are often much higher than people anticipate and they're waiting too long to save. It's important to take time to work with an advisor who's a fiduciary—someone who is legally and ethically obligated to always put you first. You need a tailor, that financial advisor, to make your plan fit your life."

What happened to the comfortable American retirement of generations past? Over the last 50 years, our country began a quiet retirement transition. It was so silent that no one paid much attention. Those days of retirees leaving the workforce with a gold watch and a pension guaranteed for life were truly the Good Old Days. Unfortunately, that train left the station a long time ago. They are gone forever, unless you work in the public sector.

Starting around 1978, Congress allowed for 401(k) plans. These new retirement accounts were intended to give employees options for retirement savings other than standard pension plans. The shift away from pensions by employers has grown ever since.

The responsibility for retirement planning has undergone a generational shift from employers to employees. The change from defined benefits plans (guaranteed pensions) to defined contribution plans [401(k) plans] has been a rocky transition at best. It has become easier for employees to ignore retirement saving for tomorrow in order to spend on consumption today.

With retirement lasting from 20–30 years for many people, what are some of the factors facing employees today?

- Americans are healthier and living longer.
- Saving for retirement happens less frequently, if at all.
- Social Security benefits alone are NOT enough to ensure a comfortable retirement. In 2020, the average annual payout for Social Security was $18,036.00. Will this amount support your lifestyle?
- Medicare will not cover the costs of assisted living or time confined to a nursing home. It only covers 100 days of care at a skilled nursing facility, if a hospital stay of three days or more preceded it. Healthcare costs continue to escalate.

Let's take a look at the large number of retirees of the Baby Boomer generation currently entering retirement age. This cohort includes those born between 1946 and 1964. Some 10,000 Baby Boomers turn 65 everyday.

Nearly half of all Baby Boomers (47%) are already retired. That totals some 34,000,000 people. They have faced these common problems in retirement:

- Too little savings.
- Underestimated healthcare costs, particularly for long-term care.
- Unrealistic expectations of how much retirement income they will need.
- Being the first generation to face saving for retirement on their own.

Traditionally, retirement planning involved creating a three-legged stool for funding consisting of:

1. Social Security benefits
2. Private pension plan
3. Personal savings

What happens when two of the three legs are missing or are grossly underfunded? If there is no private pension plan and personal savings are underfunded, the stool topples over and, with it, retirement becomes a lot less comfortable. The only options left in retirement then become undesirable:

- Downsize, adopt a lower-budget lifestyle, and try to live on Social Security benefits as your only income.
- Keep working and pass up retirement until your health fails.
- Ask family for financial assistance; become dependent on others.

These options provide a lot less funds than the Golden Years most Americans seek in retirement. Once again, experience proves to be the best teacher, but the tuition is high! Saving early, often, and regularly for retirement offers a pathway to building a comfortable nest egg. This is a crisis that can be avoided.

The general outlook for retirement for many Americans is dim given this discussion. The crisis is the clear and unsurprising result of a lack of planning. Addressing this lack of planning is the focus of this book, because a comfortable retirement is within the reach of almost anyone with a well-developed plan.

Making money decisions when the future is unclear is always difficult. The economic shutdown that began with the arrival of the coronavirus pandemic in the spring of 2020 has led to layoffs and job losses, emergency account withdrawals, and many other painful financial challenges. It has led to a surge of uncertainty and nervousness about the future.

Many people feel unsure about investing in the stock market at the present time. Others worry about job security, the wellbeing of family members, and the sustainability of their savings over time. These concerns lead to hesitation about making any longer-term financial decisions for fear that the health crisis will drag on.

While the pandemic is unprecedented for everyone, market volatility is not. Consider enlisting the help of a financial advisor (CFP/CFA) to offer some clarity on your personal financial matters. Market volatility can be unnerving, but an advisor can walk you through the pros and cons of investing and help you make financial decisions that best meet your individual requirements.

Give yourself permission to make decisions, even if they turn out to be less than perfect. This is easier said than done. However, making financial decisions while less than 50 years of age gives you many years to make up for any mistakes.

Finding a way to move forward financially in uncertain times can be one way to push past the fear of doing nothing. This pandemic, like past healthcare crises, will pass, and you need to continue moving forward to reach your retirement goals. The old saying, "If you're standing still, you're running backwards" is so true when it comes to retirement planning.

Deciding at what age to retire is a major life decision. It is a challenging and sometimes unsettling time. Many who face the question of when to retire face self-imposed pressure from their families to retire on time—whatever that means for them.

This is the estimated population breakdown by generation within the U.S.:

- Baby Boomers – born from 1946–1964; estimated 69.5 million.
- Generation X – born from 1965–1980; estimated 65.2 million.
- Millennials – born from 1981–1996; estimated 72.1 million.
- Generation Z – born from 1997–2012; estimated 67.1 million.

Within these generational cohorts, there are many different issues and available financial products offering solutions. The younger generations face a different financial landscape than our parents or even our current generation did at the same age. Unprecedented levels of student debt and soaring home prices mean there is a need to tweak the personal financial playbook.

If you have high levels of debt when you start your career, pay off high interest, non-deductible debt first, such as credit cards, then move on to paying down lower-interest debt such as student loans or a home mortgage. Personal savings and investment may only involve small amounts to start, but it is important to start the savings habit early.

Eventually, most of us will trade in going to work everyday for some form of retirement. Will *you* ever retire? If you have funded your retirement plan along the way, you will have options on what to do next after a long career.

What if you don't *want* to retire? If you want to work into your 70s, 80s, or even 90s, studies have shown not retiring can be emotionally, physically, and financially rewarding. Working gives people a sense of purpose, and by working longer, you can save more.

In their paper "The Power of Working Longer," authors G. Bronshtein, J. Scott, J. Shoven, and S. Slavov report that those saving for retirement would be better off working longer than just increasing their savings. "Delaying retirement by 3–6 months has the same impact on the retirement standard of living as saving an additional one percentage point of earnings for 30 years." If you choose not to retire, that might be a good decision for you; however, it is not for everyone. Furthermore, it's quite possible to save considerably more than several months of your salary-and I'm going to walk you through how to do just that.

Here are three things you can do to make sure you'll be ready to retire to a life free of financial worries.

1. Save an adequate amount for an emergency fund. I recommend six months of living expenses or more.
2. Work with a financial professional to develop a comprehensive plan for retirement. Go to www.NAPFA.org to find a financial advisor in your area, or ask friends for advisor referrals.

AND/OR:

3. Design your own plan, creating a design-it-yourself (DIY) solution for a comfortable retirement.

In today's uncertain world caused by the coronavirus pandemic, it's more important than ever to have some type of plan for retirement. Be intentional and focused, and develop a multifaceted approach to achieve your long-term goals. If you just look to the past, you will lose sight of the future.

It doesn't matter whether you work with a financial professional or design it yourself (DIY). The key is to develop a plan that works best for you and your family. In this book, I'll share advice of a general nature, but it cannot address the specific circumstances of any individual. You must make the choices that are right for you, creating a retirement plan tailored to your personal needs.

There's a clear need for retirement solutions. However, creating secure retirement plans for everyday investors is entirely possible with advanced planning.

I want to offer a quick word of explanation about the title of this book, *PATHWAY TO A PENSION: Follow My Rules of Engagement to a Lifetime Retirement Paycheck*. This book envisions the everyday investor's journey, following along a footpath to a final destination. Successful retirement planning requires following a series of steps to achieve your retirement goals. Rules of engagement normally signify a military authority's directive that determines when its troops can engage in combat, according to the Oxford English Dictionary. I use the term "rules of engagement" in a non-military manner. My intention is to provide a framework or set of rules to follow in preparation of your personal pension plan. I strongly believe employees and everyday investors should take responsibility for their own actions and hold themselves accountable for their own behavior when it comes to providing for a financially secure retirement. Following my rules of engagement can lead to this positive outcome.

The publication in your hands is a countercultural force in today's world of consumerism and demand for instant gratification. We are at war—with ourselves, with the passage of time, with our society, and with the "I want it **ALL**, I want it **NOW**" culture. Too many Americans focus only on the short-term rather than the longer-term needed for retirement planning success. This short-term thinking will undermine the economic security needed in retirement.

I am committed to helping you improve the financial outcomes of your retirement in ways that are most beneficial to you. Let me show you the pathway forward to building your personal pension plan by following my rules of engagement. You can retire successfully with a lifetime paycheck by following these financial strategies. Most good things in life are pretty simple. Are you ready for a custom-made personal pension plan? Let's get started investing in your future.

CHAPTER ONE

WHAT WENT WRONG?

After a 45-year career as a machinist for a mid-sized family-owned business, Harold reluctantly found himself at his own retirement party. He was not in a celebratory mood, however.

Life comes at you fast. The years had flown by. He had raised a family alongside his wife of 40 years, bought and paid for a house and two cars, and seen their two children graduate from college without incurring student loans. Harold was debt-averse. He had provided financially for his family but had neglected focusing on his own retirement planning.

Like many people his age, Harold had the benefit of a SEP IRA established by his employer. In a SEP IRA, only the employer can contribute to the plan. There are no voluntary contributions. These plans are similar to a profit-sharing plan because contributions can be made at the discretion of the employer. The company had averaged a 3% of salary contribution to the plan for Harold over the past 10 years.

Harold had never invested in other retirement alternatives, as he did not feel comfortable with his lack of knowledge about the stock market and finance in general. He believed his SEP IRA account would be enough to provide for a comfortable retirement fund. After all, retirement had always seemed a long way in the distance.

The SEP IRA was the only investment Harold had maintained consistently toward his retirement. The bulk of his earnings went toward living expenses and supporting his family. He did have a savings account balance of $12,000.

Harold had the illusion of wealth when he looked at the balance of his retirement fund. He felt reassured by the size of the balance in the fund when he received his annual statement of benefits summary. Like many of his contemporaries, Harold had thought a balance of $100,000 was sufficient. However, when he was told that the lump sum of that account translates into approximately $500 a month in retirement, that savings balance seemed much less sufficient.

At retirement, Harold found the balance in his SEP IRA account was well short of an amount he would need to support his lifestyle for the next 20–30 years. Harold had run out of time to fund his retirement in order to provide for a comfortable departure from the workforce. Where had Harold gone wrong?

Harold's story is an important reminder to calculate a retiree's savings in terms of projected monthly income, not just total assets. This approach gives people a better sense of whether they need to save more or work longer to maintain their standard of living in retirement. This calculation should be made at least annually, during the accumulation phase of building a retirement fund.

Harold violated my basic rule of thumb for budgeting by never allocating any of his after-tax income toward retirement. This rule-of-thumb budget approach was designed for budgeters who lack the patience for tracking their spending in more detailed categories and who need guidance to put aside funds for retirement. It is too much to expect busy people to track every income and expense item to the penny; I therefore developed this shorthand budget approach that I call my 50-20-30 plan.

My 50-20-30 plan works like this. With each month's after-tax income, a basic allocation is made as follows:

- 50% is allocated for living expenses.
- 20% is allocated for discretionary expenses.
- 30% is allocated for saving and investing along with debt reduction.

For example, if your monthly after-tax income were $6,000, the allocation would look like this:

- 50% or $3,000 for living expenses.
- 20% or $1,200 for discretionary spending.
- 30% or $1,800 for saving and debt reduction.

Over time, as debt is reduced, more funds can be allocated for saving and investing. There will be months when these numbers are in excess of your spending needs within these categories, and this can also be a source of additional funds for investing. I will share more detailed information on my budgeting plan in Part Two.

After six months in retirement, Harold decided to return to the workforce. Last I heard, he was working part-time for a machine repair shop as a way to supplement his retirement income. He is another example of the woulda, coulda, shoulda generation wishing they had saved more for retirement. Hope really is not a strategy!

Harold was also a victim of exponential growth bias. Say you have a penny that doubles in value every day. How much money will you have after 31 days?

For most people, their number is far below the actual answer. You will have more than $10 million after 31 days of doubling.

Although the math is basic arithmetic, many adults assume the answer will be far smaller. This error in calculations is known as exponential growth bias, or EGB. EGB is the tendency to neglect the effects of compound interest, which happens when earned interest is reinvested over time.

The lesson to be learned from understanding exponential growth bias is that the best way to convince people to save more is to help them understand the reality of compounding, which is the magic that happens to their money when they invest and leave it alone over time. Harold waited too long to recover from a form of exponential growth bias, as he assumed his savings would be adequate for retirement.

Ultimately, what went wrong was Harold's failure to estimate how much money he would need in retirement. Had he made an effort to estimate this amount early in his career, he would have known he needed to accumulate more than what was in his SEP IRA account at his retirement party.

CHAPTER TWO

THE SMELL OF MONEY

If you could provide your family with $1,000,000 of financial security, why would you pass up this opportunity? Yet this is what many working Americans do in reality.

One way to give your family this level of financial security is through a term life insurance policy. For as little as $1 per day, it is possible to purchase a $1,000,000 term policy naming your spouse or trust as the beneficiary. Upon your death, the insurance company pays out the death benefit of $1,000,000 to your named beneficiary.

These are the approximate numbers for a 30-year-old male in good health. This level of death benefits could go a long way in providing for a young, growing family if he were to suffer an early death. This is what providing financial security looks like. Let's hope you never have to call upon the term life insurance policy, but it will give you peace of mind just in case.

Shopping for a term life insurance policy is easy. You can talk with your insurance agent about policy options they offer or go on the Internet and find term life insurance premium quotes from multiple companies. It is easy to compare the costs of various term policies. Try www.NerdWallet.com/lifeinsurance for a source of premium quotes.

Having a term life insurance policy is a risk-mitigation strategy that can offer peace of mind if you become ill and pass away prematurely while your family is young and dependent on you as the primary wage earner.

In addition to a term policy that will cover the risk of an early death, a second way to provide financial security for your family is to develop a well-funded retirement plan that will provide another level of peace of mind from financial worries. It is reasonable to project that you can build a $1,000,000 retirement fund if you start early, follow my Rules of Engagement, and stay the course. More details on my Rules of Engagement will follow in Part Two.

Some 300 years ago, in 1720, "the scent of money was in the air like the breath of spring," as the historian John Carswell put it. That June, eighty-eight (88) startups, most of them publicly traded, were launched in London. This surge in fundraising probably created one of the earliest financial bubbles. Financial bubbles are neither rational nor irrational; they are profoundly human-driven, and they continue to occur century after century. There is something about human nature that makes us fear missing out on the next big thing. If everyone else is making money on an idea, we want to be a part of it. This is one example of groupthink.

I am not talking about financial bubbles in this context. Rather, I use the smell of money as a metaphor for the benefits derived from hard work, focused saving and investing, and personal perseverance to achieve a financial goal. It is not an unpleasant odor, but rather, the sweet smell of prosperity and a bright future.

While growing up, I spent my summers working on my grandfather's farm. My memories of those summers always bring an emotional tug of nostalgia. My grandfather raised row crops like wheat, corn, and soybeans. He also had acreage dedicated to prairie hay and pasture land. He always had a cow-calf operation, with calves being fattened for the market. He was a successful farmer/rancher his entire life.

On certain days, the cattle feedlot closest to the house gave off a strong, pungent odor, depending on the direction of the wind. Anytime I complained of this odor, my uncle would comment, "That is the smell of money. Follow that scent to success." As I grew older, I understood his statement better. This was my first encounter with the smell of money.

After college, I served on active duty in the Army for more than four years. I was an officer in the Army Finance Corps. Part of my job during those years of service involved preparing and disbursing monthly payrolls. The Army paid in cash with denominations from $1 to $20 for those soldiers being paid after their allotments were sent by check to bank accounts, parents, wives, and other designated beneficiaries.

The largest cash payrolls I worked on totaled more than $20,000,000. That's a lot of cash to verify and divide into multiple smaller payrolls for distribution at the individual company level. This offered me another example of the smell of money. It was a very distinctive odor.

On my way to earning an MBA degree in finance, I worked part-time as a bank teller and supervised the cash vault of a bank. Again, this involved verifying large sums of cash and disbursing cash daily to each teller. The smell of money was always in the air and on my hands.

As my career in banking progressed, I developed my personal retirement plan and funded it over the years following my Rules of Engagement. The sweet smell of money was evident each year as I approached retirement and achieved my retirement fund goals.

As you can see, the smell of money played a significant role in my career and helped me stay on course to achieve my retirement goals. It is possible for you to do the same thing during your career. What is the source of the smell of money for you, conjuring the sweet scent of successful retirement planning?

I was fortunate that my career was in banking. I worked around money and various financial dealings for over 40 years. The $1,000,000 in financial security discussed earlier in this chapter is not only a nice round number; it also provides a dollar goal to aspire to achieve. After all, it is very difficult to hit a target if you don't have one!

CHAPTER THREE

MOVING PAST THE GOOD OLD DAYS

Like most adults, you probably fall into one of two broad categories when it comes to retirement planning, characterized by two types of thinking:

1. I do not want to run out of money or be a burden to anyone when I retire. I have developed a plan to meet my financial retirement goals. I want to arrive at the intersection where work is optional because I know I have sufficient funds to retire.
2. Retirement is a long way off, and I have more pressing financial needs to deal with than worrying about retirement some 30 years in the future. I will address retirement planning later, when I have more time and more money.

Congratulations, if you are in the group described in #1. You are well on your way to a successful retirement. If you fall into the group described in #2, you are headed for a potential financial crisis and a major disappointment that can be avoided. Delaying retirement planning is a curse, not a viable strategy.

Regardless of which category you find yourself in, there are at least three critical questions that must ultimately be answered by both groups:

1. Can I afford to retire?
2. How much money will I need in retirement?
3. How can I meet my retirement financial goals?

Breaking up is never easy, and Americans' love affair with a corporate pension plan is ending due to the dramatic change in availability of such plans, with unpleasant consequences. The change from a defined-benefits pension plan (a specified payment for life or a lump sum upon retirement) to a defined contribution plan [a 401(k), 403(b), or 457 plan] has direct consequences for all employees.

The traditional pension plan was designed to reward loyal employees for their long years of service to a single company. In effect, pensions were a form of golden handcuffs, tying employer and employee together for the duration of a career. These employer-sponsored plans had numerous pros and cons. Here is a short list of those features.

PROS AND CONS OF PENSIONS

ADVANTAGES	DISADVANTAGES
No investment risk for employee	No investment control for employee
Monthly payments for life	No early access to funds
Some tax benefits on contributions	Lack of flexibility
Guaranteed by the Pension Benefit Guaranty Corp	Complications of plans

A defined contribution plan is a retirement plan in which an employee, employer, or both contributes money. Future benefits fluctuate on the basis of investment earnings. Today, employer-sponsored defined contribution plans are the most widely used type of retirement benefit plans [401(k) plans].

Employees voluntarily choose to invest a portion of their salaries in these defined contribution plans to build their retirement funds in order to supplement future Social Security benefits. The employee decides how much to invest, with these contributions deducted from their paycheck. Contributions are limited by IRS guidelines. Employees also choose the types of investments to make from those offered by the plan.

Employees can make withdrawals from their defined contribution plans beginning at age 59 ½ without penalty. Withdrawals prior to this age carry heavy penalties. Employee contributions are pre-tax and grow in the plan on a tax-deferred basis until withdrawn. Taking full advantage of tax-deferred investing is key to building a retirement fund more quickly.

As you can see, just like a landline for your home phone or floppy discs for your computer, corporate-sponsored pension plans are largely a relic of the past. This has exacerbated retirement insecurity, or what I call Pension Envy. This is where the perception of not having the safety net of a pension, or defined benefits plan, continues to haunt many who are approaching retirement today.

The most common employment group who still has access to a defined benefit plan (a pension) is public sector employees. If you work as a teacher, firefighter, or police officer, or if you work for a city, state, or federal agency, you may still have a defined benefits plan. These defined retirement benefits allow these employees to plan their income levels in retirement with some certainty. This comfort level is not available to the majority of employees in the private sector. Pension envy is alive and growing!

One answer to pension envy is developing a way to survive the coming retirement crisis. A solution will involve more saving by individuals along with better financial education. Financial literacy needs to improve for the general public. With financial literacy comes a clearer understanding of the need to save and how to invest. Financial literacy is critical to provide individuals with the knowledge and tools to develop and sustain a solid financial foundation.

Retirees face a double whammy: generating adequate income AND paying for long-term healthcare. For many, working longer to put off retirement will help their financial situation, but working longer CANNOT be an alternative to saving. Working longer may not be an option for some facing forced early retirement, health issues preventing work, the natural loss of energy and physical stamina that comes with aging, and the potential of being out of work and unemployable before retirement age. If any of these events occur, it can create a desperate situation for a person without health insurance who is facing a coverage gap before Medicare becomes available at age 65. This is the worst of all possible situations.

In these unfortunate cases, having a personal pension plan to help bridge the gap to eligibility for Medicare would be a welcome financial solution. Part Two will discuss how my Rules of Engagement offer winning financial strategies to help people achieve a type of financial security.

Another solution to provide funds for healthcare in your later years is to open a health savings account (HSA) today. This is a type of savings account that lets you set aside money on a pre-tax basis to pay for qualified medical expenses. HSA accounts are commonly used to pay for deductibles, copayments, coinsurance, and other medical expenses that may lower your total healthcare costs. To be eligible to open an HSA, you must have a special type of health insurance called a high-deductible plan. Funds in an HSA account roll over from year to year and can continue to grow.

There are limits to annual contributions to an HSA account. In 2021, the maximum contribution for individuals is $3,600 and $7,200 for families. The annual catch-up contribution for those over the age of 55 is $1,000.

The advantages of tax-deferred earnings and the annual roll-over provision for unused funds make an HSA a viable choice for some individuals to cover healthcare costs in retirement.

If committing to building a personal pension is beyond your interest, or if it will add to your current financial stress, you may be relegated to the sidelines while others find ways to overcome pension envy. Even worse, you may join the legions of those in the "race to the bottom" of retirement preparation. I recommend you work with a financial advisor to help you achieve a lifetime retirement paycheck.

Obviously, those fortunate enough to have a pension have an advantage in retirement income, as they may have four sources of income: Social Security, pension income, dividends and interest, and withdrawals from IRAs and other investments. Without a pension, the income sources shrink to three: Social Security, dividends and interest, and withdrawals from other investments.

Without a pension, most choices for everyday investors will default to the following:

- Focusing on more income-producing investments.
- Downsizing by moving to more affordable housing and using the equity from the sale of your home for investments.

- Saving more during your working years.
- Planning on working longer, maybe to age 75 or beyond.

A personal pension is only one component of a total retirement plan. See Chapter Twelve for a more detailed discussion of the multiple components that I believe make up a complete retirement plan.

If you don't have a retirement plan, you are not alone. The state where you live might be working on solving that problem for you. According to data from the National Institute on Retirement Security, 59% of working-age people in America don't have any money in a retirement account—whether an employer-sponsored 401(k) or an IRA—and aren't covered by any defined-benefit pensions. For those who do have a retirement account, most have balances smaller than their annual income.

Ten states have recently passed legislation creating programs designed to get more people enrolled in retirement plans, and additional states are considering similar actions. These states recognize the coming retirement crisis and are doing something to help prevent it in order to alleviate funding pressure that they could incur in the future.

States are considering three types of plans: an auto-enrolled IRA, a marketplace, and a multi-employer plan. This is an evolving area of retirement planning, and I encourage you to check with your state of residency for the latest developments where you live.

The best cure for pension envy is to build your own personal pension plan. Short of this solution, the only other realistic cure for pension envy is more savings!

A pension sounds complicated, but it has a simple purpose: to provide you with a lifetime income. This steady income can provide the financial security needed for your retirement years. However, pensions are different from savings. You do not outlive a pension, while savings may run out!

Those nearing retirement age face many negative consequences if they don't take action now. Without taking proactive measures to correct their course, younger participants will become part of the statistical analysis of what went wrong with retirement planning in the next few decades.

It does not have to end this way. If more people will self-educate themselves in financial literacy by getting their financial lives in order, they can focus on building a comfortable retirement nest egg. Following my Rules of Engagement outlined in Part Two of this book will guide most people to the on-ramp to retirement solutions that can contribute to a more robust financial future.

Moving past the good old days can be a meaningful elevation in thinking about retirement, uplifting rather than sad. The future holds new opportunities for all of us. Better retirement planning is just one of those opportunities.

PART TWO

MY RULES OF ENGAGEMENT: SEVEN WINNING FINANCIAL STRATEGIES

CHAPTER FOUR

RULE #1

50-20-30 BUDGET PLAN

My first rule of engagement on the way to building a financially secure retirement plan is to adopt my 50-20-30 budgeting plan. Until you understand your current income and expense history, it is very difficult to plan for the future. To plan any journey, you must start with your current location (your current income and expense numbers) to determine how to arrive at your final destination (your retirement goal). My 50-20-30 plan will help you map out a workable savings plan, regardless of your income level.

Budgeting is a simple approach to allow you to live within your income. It is not time-consuming, and it will get you started on your way to building a retirement fund.

Achieving success with a big financial goal starts with small steps. Budgeting is the first step. Having a positive attitude about saving is important, along with the desire to save some amount monthly, regardless of how much you earn.

When you receive your next monthly paycheck or automatic deposit to your account, record the net-pay amount as the pool of funds available to manage in paying all of your expenses for the month. My budgeting plan will give you an allocation process for the major categories of expenses such as utilities, insurance, rent or mortgage payments, food, and other living expenses.

My 50-20-30 budgeting plan works like this. Fifty percent (50%) of net pay is allocated for living expenses; twenty percent (20%) goes toward discretionary expenses like dining out, a movie, cable TV, and dry cleaning; and another thirty percent (30%) is left for debt reduction, saving, and investing.

Summarize your expenses into these three categories and list the detailed amount of each bill in the appropriate one. The spreadsheet for the month might look like this:

EXAMPLE SPREADSHEET FOR JOHN SAMPLE
BUDGETING 50-20-30
January 2021

Net Pay	Living Expenses	Discretionary Funds	Debt Reduction/ Saving
$1,850	Rent: $750	Date night: $200	Left over: $40
	Utilities: $185	Cable TV: $100	
	Food: $400	Misc: $50	
	Insurance: $125		
	Total: $1,460	Total: $350	Total: $40

At first glance, this expense summary indicates that John Sample needs help. His living expenses total 79% of his net pay, his discretionary expenses are 19%, and funds placed into debt and savings only represent 2%.

Without making any adjustments to his current spending, John Sample has only $40 a month to make debt reductions and/or save! Most likely, John also has a car payment or other debt not listed here that he must service monthly. If this is the case, he is underwater every month.

I recommend that John reduce his living expenses by seeking a roommate to share rent and utility costs. I also recommend dropping cable TV unless the roommate will share in these expenses as well. Streaming on a computer could be a cheaper way to watch movies and the news. Date night expenses could also be reduced. These changes should get him to the break-even point or perhaps provide a small amount of money to begin saving.

If you are in debt and feel like you cannot save, a solution is readily available. The solution to getting out of debt and starting to save and fund your retirement goals is putting yourself on a budget and sticking with it.

Saving starts with the desire to save rather than spending everything you make. If you can make the conscious decision to save something from every paycheck, you are on your way to implementing Rule #2. Work at achieving the 50-20-30 split over time.

A simplistic budget plan can help track past expenses and current spending. It can also offer guidance on how to allocate your earnings going forward and provide the funding sources for more effective retirement funding.

CHAPTER FIVE

RULE #2

BUILD AN EMERGENCY FUND

Rule #2 is as simple as following the advice given by your parents and grandparents when you were still living at home. Keep some cash available for unknown expenses! It is necessary to establish and maintain an emergency fund, sometimes called a rainy day fund. This is a safety net for future unknown needs. If you don't provide for your emergencies, who will?

The dollar amount to be saved in an emergency fund varies according to your lifestyle. A generally accepted amount is 3–6 months of living expenses. Keep these funds in a money market account earning interest. You might as well get paid while holding these funds in a safe, secure place for emergency use.

Wherever you keep these funds, they need to be liquid. Never park these funds in any type of account that can go down in value or that will charge a fee for withdrawals. After all, you are saving for the unexpected in this account. Who knows when or how often you may need to draw on these funds?

My personal recommendation is to build an emergency fund equal to six months of living expenses. This stash of cash is set aside to cover the larger financial surprises that life invariably throws our way. These unexpected events can be stressful and costly. Here are a few examples of unknown expenses people might encounter:

- Loss of a job
- Medical or dental emergency for you or a family member
- Major home appliance repair or replacement
- Significant car repairs
- Roof repairs or replacement
- Furnace or air conditioner repair or replacement
- Pet emergency
- Need to take unpaid leave to serve as a caregiver for an ailing parent or relative

Having an emergency fund offers peace of mind by keeping you prepared for life's surprises. It will also offer comfort by ensuring that you will not have to go into debt, or add to your debt, if an emergency arises.

There are many ways to build an emergency fund. Some of the most reliable techniques include the following:

- Determine the total you want to save in your fund and set that amount as a goal.
- Set a monthly savings amount to reach this total goal within two years.
- Keep the change when you get one- and five-dollar bills after breaking a $10 or $20. Drop some of this change in a jar at home and when the jar is full, take it to the bank.
- Save any tax refund.
- Set up an automatic transfer from your checking account into this emergency fund on a monthly basis.
- Deposit any monetary gifts or retail purchase refunds into this account, as these are one-off opportunities to save.

After you have determined a dollar number as a goal for your emergency fund, and before you begin saving, I recommend you first pay down high-interest-rate credit card debt. Any interest rate of 10% or more should be your first target to eliminate. The second step is to develop a spending plan within the framework of my 50-20-30 budget plan. Third, plan on starting small by making incremental deposit amounts into your new fund. Do not let the destination or ultimate size of the fund overwhelm you. Start small and build from there.

Here is an example: If you have determined you need a $10,000 contingency fund, here is one way to achieve that amount.

- Make an initial investment of $2,500.
- Add $200 per month.
- Have an interest rate on your savings account of 1.0%.
- After 3 years, the account value is $9,881.

Like so many projects in life, just getting started in building an emergency fund is a big step forward in reaching your ultimate milestone of a fully funded retirement account. Start saving today.

Turning to a credit card to handle a financial emergency is NOT a good alternative for a rainy day fund. You need to have a cash buffer to avoid a feeling of panic and the need to go further into debt because of an unexpected expense.

Everyone, regardless of income level, needs an emergency fund. Perhaps a better name for this fund would be a *contingency account*. Not every expense paid out of this account will be defined as an emergency.

The 2020 pandemic provided a clear example of the importance of having funds set aside for unknown expenses. Reduced or lost wages from many employment categories has forced a majority of Americans to fall back on their savings to sustain themselves during the pandemic. Those with a funded emergency account are thankful; those without such a fund now understand the need to establish one going forward.

Put your plan into action and grow your fund toward the goal you have set. As you draw on the fund for unexpected expenses, plan to replenish the account. This contingency fund is a fundamental requirement for a secure lifestyle and retirement. When your fund is underway, you are ready to continue on with my Rules of Engagement.

CHAPTER SIX

RULE #3

DECIDE WHETHER TO PAY OFF MORTGAGE EARLY

Rule #3 is to pay off your mortgage sooner rather than later (or not at all). My preference for taking action on this rule has changed over time as the income tax code has changed. With an increase in the standard deduction allowed on a personal federal tax return to the current $12,550 for a single filer and $25,100 for a married couple filing a joint return, for many people, it may make less economic sense to claim itemized deductions.

With the increased standard deduction, claiming mortgage interest paid as an itemized deduction may be less valuable than it used to be. Thus, with the loss of the deductibility of mortgage interest, it may be best to pay off that home mortgage sooner rather than later. If it's not deductible, pay it off!

For years, I used mortgage interest as one of my largest itemized deductions. Making mortgage payments made sense, as the interest deduction lowered my overall tax bill. This changed starting with the 2019 tax return when itemized deductions became less important with the increase in the standard deductions available to all income tax filers.

Rule #3 has evolved as a result of this change in tax policy. Paying a mortgage off early may make sense for some but not for everyone. If your itemized deductions exceed the standard deduction, then continue to make your regular mortgage payments. If you are a savvy investor and can invest excess funds at a higher return than your mortgage interest rate, it may make sense to stay on schedule with your mortgage. More on this later.

Application of Rule #3 is arbitrary because each family's situation is unique. Run the numbers and decide which approach is best for you. This is one area of personal finance where one size **does not** fit everyone.

Sometimes the final decision on implementing this rule is not just about the numbers. Many couples are very uncomfortable with having any mortgage. Any debt adds stress to their marriage. For them, paying off the mortgage is as much about stress release as it is a financial decision. Other couples find comfort in having larger balances in their bank accounts, and paying off the mortgage early would reduce those cash balances. Deciding which mortgage approach works for you truly is a balancing act.

Here are the advantages I see in paying off a mortgage early. I think these apply to the majority of people, although this is a case-by-case decision.

ADVANTAGES OF EARLY MORTGAGE PAYOFF

1. Potentially reducing your income taxes, as discussed above. If the interest is not deductible, pay off the mortgage sooner rather than later.
2. Gaining peace of mind due to a desire to be debt-free, excitement of meeting a financial goal of being debt-free, or less stress in a marriage.

3. Improving monthly cash flow, which makes more funds available for investments. When a mortgage is paid in full, it is like earning a risk-free return equal to the mortgage interest rate.

4. Increasing savings and investments.

Most mortgages do not have pre-payment penalties; therefore, depending on how you prepay your mortgage, no fees may be required.

Many times I am asked how to pay off a mortgage early when families have other equally pressing living expenses. The easy answer is, "It's all about choices." The choices we make about how we spend money and when we spend it are the foundations of budgeting. Eating out frequently versus preparing meals at home; driving the family car another three to five years rather than trading it in to enjoy all the options available on a newer model; and living within your means without incurring credit card debt are all examples of choices we can all make that affect our available funds for debt-reduction and investing.

Adults like to have a template to follow when they undertake a new project or pursue a goal. If you're looking for a more granular methodology for paying off a mortgage sooner rather than later, here are four proven methods to paying off a mortgage early. Always check with your mortgage lender before you make any payment changes to ensure your lender permits them.

FOUR METHODS TO ACCELERATE PAYMENTS ON A MORTGAGE

MAKE PERIODIC EXTRA PAYMENTS: This is the easiest method and the one where an individual can be in full control. Make the extra payments when you have excess cash and skip them when you don't. Most mortgage lenders and mortgage service companies allow extra principal payments.

If you choose to make extra payments, here are two ways to structure them. First, split your regular monthly payment in half and make bi-weekly payments. The total dollar amount of payments remains the same as your existing mortgage payments, but you effectively make 13 payments annually versus 12 following the one-payment-per-month approach. This extra payment concept works because you are accelerating the principal reduction with each bi-weekly payment.

The second way to make extra payments is to pay more each month to reduce your principal faster. For example, if your mortgage balance is $250,000 with a 30-year maturity and has a 4.0% interest rate, an additional $100 per month will save four years on the maturity and $27,957 on the total mortgage. Making the extra monthly payment of $100 offers flexibility. You decide when you want to make the extra payment and when you don't. The contractual monthly payment amount required remains unchanged.

REFINANCE: With interest rates at historic lows, many homeowners are refinancing to lower their payments and lock in low mortgage rates. The advantage of refinancing is a lower interest rate and a savings in total interest paid over the life of the mortgage. Refinancing has fees associated with the paperwork, so be sure your savings in monthly payments is not lost to the cost of the refinancing fees.

I encourage you to consider lowering the maturity of your mortgage, if you are considering refinancing. Moving from a 30-year mortgage to a 15-year maturity will save a lot of interest over the life of the mortgage.

RECAST YOUR MORTGAGE: This method is not as popular as refinancing, and it requires an advance agreement from your mortgage lender. Recasting a mortgage involves keeping your current mortgage in place while making lump-sum payments toward the principal. The lender adjusts the amortization to reflect the new balance after each payment. This method is not available to VA or FHA loans.

The advantage of recasting is usually lower fees than a refinance. Some lenders require lump-sum payments in $5,000 minimum increments to recast the mortgage. The ultimate benefit of recasting is lower monthly payments, as the payments are recalculated after each lump-sum payment. In a lump-sum payment method without recasting, the monthly payments stay the same.

MAKE LUMP-SUM PAYMENTS AGAINST THE PRINCIPAL: Making periodic lump-sum payments on an existing mortgage is another flexible approach to reducing your mortgage faster. This method works well for those who are self-employed and others who might receive quarterly payments from their business such as a bonus or profit-sharing distribution. Other sources of lump-sum payments might include an inheritance, proceeds from the sale of an asset like a rental property, or the sale of any other asset.

Whatever method of these four works best for you, it will save you money over time that can be used for other purposes. I do not recommend accelerating mortgage reductions until after you have taken care of these essential financial priorities:

- Pay off high-interest credit card debt.
- Make investing for retirement a priority by automating your contributions.
- Build an emergency fund (contingency fund).

Not everyone agrees that paying off a mortgage early is ultimately beneficial. There is a contrarian strategy characterized by maintaining your mortgage on regular payments and investing to earn a higher yield than the mortgage interest rate. This strategy requires financial discipline to really work. This alternate strategy works like this:

- Refinance your mortgage to the lowest rate you qualify for.
- Use the delta—the difference between the original mortgage rate and the refinanced rate—to invest every month in a taxable account; automate the monthly transfer of funds.
- Buy a different dividend-paying stock each month for a year.
- After a year, continue to invest the delta among these same stocks and build a sizable position in them over time.
- Reinvest the dividends using a DRIP program.

This strategy is relevant because we are currently in a historically low-interest-rate market AND the stocks you select should be those that pay a yield higher than your refinanced mortgage rate.

Using this alternative strategy will offer an opportunity to build an income portfolio over time. All funds should be left in this portfolio and allowed to compound. This strategy should help you build wealth faster IF you maintain the financial discipline to invest regularly and leave this portfolio alone until retirement. Not everyone has this discipline, and for this group, paying off the mortgage sooner is a better option.

When the three essential financial priorities have been completed as outlined in this chapter, it is time to focus on either paying off the mortgage early or funding a diversified dividend-oriented portfolio, if you have the financial discipline. Either strategy will result in offering you more financial flexibility.

CHAPTER SEVEN

RULE #4

529 SAVING PLAN

Rule #4 applies if you have a family and you want your children to attend private schools and/or college. Saving for educational expenses using a 529 plan is my Rule #4. The name 529 comes from Section 529 of the Internal Revenue Code, which authorized these "qualified tuition plans."

Whether you and your spouse want to provide your children with 100% funding for college, cover a partial amount of the cost, or just make a token contribution toward this higher education goal, saving money in a 529 plan makes good economic sense. Investing in your children's future is every parent's dream and can be accomplished with a little research.

The 529 Saving Plan is a tax-advantaged investment account designed to encourage saving for educational expenses for a designated beneficiary. These plans are **not** just for college expenses. They can be used for tuition and other educational expenses for K–12 in addition to college expenses. With state tax benefits available in some states and federal tax savings available everywhere for these contributions, these benefits should make 529 plans an integral part of your education funding strategy.

The federal tax savings occur as long as the money stays in the account, as no income taxes will be due on earnings. When money is withdrawn for qualified educational expenses, those withdrawals may be federal income tax-free and, in many cases, free of state taxes as well.

If your state of residency does not offer a 529 plan, you can choose a plan from certain other states. There are some 30 states offering a state income tax deduction or state tax credit for contributions to a 529 plan from residents of their state. Any U.S. resident age 18 or over with a Social Security number may open a 529 plan account. Anyone of any age with a Social Security number may be a beneficiary of these accounts. Children and grandchildren are the most common beneficiaries.

An even broader tax benefit is offered by seven states that allow for state tax benefits for contributions made to any 529 plan anywhere in the U.S. For example, if you are a resident of Kansas and you choose a 529 plan offered by Florida, you still qualify for state tax benefits in Kansas. Here is the list of those seven states:

1. Arizona
2. Arkansas
3. Kansas
4. Minnesota
5. Missouri
6. Montana
7. Pennsylvania

Parents and grandparents of the beneficiary are usually the sources of funding for these educational accounts. Gifting money to an existing 529 plan account may offer some estate planning benefits. Check with your tax professional on this matter.

Investment options include age-based investment strategies managed professionally by companies like Fidelity, Schwab, and Vanguard. Withdrawals can be made at any time for qualified educational expenses. If the withdrawals are spent on non-qualified expenses, penalties and tax payments may be due.

The account owner has full control over when and how the money is spent. The owner can change beneficiaries of the account at any time. As long as the parents are the account owner and their child is a dependent, the balance of the 529 plan account will have very little impact on financial aid applications.

There are many other ways to save for your children's educational expenses. Custodial UGMA and UTMA accounts with a bank can be used for any purpose, including education. A regular savings account in the parent's name gives maximum flexibility in how money is spent. Roth IRAs can be used for both college expenses and retirement income while still bringing tax-deferred advantages. Roth IRAs should not count as assets for financial aid. Coverdell Education Savings Accounts are tax-deferred trust accounts that can be used for K–12 and higher education expenses.

Another option for paying college tuition is to pay for it in advance with a prepaid tuition plan. There are currently 9 states that offer these plans and are open to new enrollment. In most cases, you must be a resident of the state if you want to use its prepaid tuition plan.

PREPAID TUITION PLAN STATES

1. Florida
2. Maryland
3. Massachusetts
4. Michigan
5. Mississippi

6. Nevada
7. Pennsylvania
8. Texas
9. Washington

In addition to this list of states, a number of private colleges offer some form of prepaid tuition plan.

Most prepaid plans let you pay tuition into a state fund at today's prices, then cash it in for college credits years in the future. If you are concerned about taking investment risks, these plans may be an option. But prepaid tuition plans are not for everyone. Here are some questions to ask yourself if you are considering these plans:

- Are you likely to send your child to an in-state school?
- How fast is college tuition rising in your state?
- How strongly does the state guarantee this fund?
- How will you pay for room and board, as these expenses are not covered by the prepaid plan?
- Does your child want to attend college?

If you are interested in a prepaid tuition plan, more research should be done through your financial advisor or your state education department. I would be very cautious in signing up for a prepaid plan.

Here's the bottom line: Using a tax-advantaged 529 savings plan makes a lot of sense for the majority of parents and grandparents when saving for a child's future educational needs. Make use of any tax-advantaged plan like a 529 savings plan to accelerate the accumulation of funds. The sooner you start funding these accounts, the more funds should be available for future educational expenses. Whatever you do, I encourage you to start saving early for your children's education.

CHAPTER EIGHT

RULE #5

SAVE EARLY, OFTEN, AND REGULARLY

Rule #5 is the core subject of this book. Saving early, often, and regularly for retirement is critical if you plan to retire with a comfortable nest egg.

I always remind myself of this basic financial truth: *You can borrow for college and most asset purchases, but you cannot borrow for retirement.* If you do not save and invest for your retirement, no one will come to your rescue. You are on your own!

A word of warning: You may have seen advertisements promoting reverse mortgages as a way to finance retirement. I am not a fan of these financial products, as they shrink the value of one of the primary assets in your estate, your home. If you have no other assets to support you in retirement, then using the equity in your home may be one of the only options left.

Reverse mortgages are a different type of mortgage but with diabolical twists. Like all financial products, the devil is always in the details. With a reverse mortgage, the loan balance increases over time as interest and fees on the loan accumulate, unlike a traditional mortgage whose balance reduces with each payment. Reverse mortgages typically do not require monthly payments.

As a homeowner, with a reverse mortgage, you retain title to the property but are also responsible for property taxes, insurance, maintenance, and utilities. The most common way to repay a reverse mortgage is by selling the home. These loans are usually more expensive than traditional mortgages. If you want to use the equity in your home for a loan, I recommend a home equity line of credit (HELOC) rather than a reverse mortgage. There is no free lunch.

Most of us put other family members ahead of ourselves when it comes to providing for our own financial security. If you decide to become the bank of Mom and Dad—offering financial assistance to an adult child—you could also be sacrificing your retirement security. **MAKE FUNDING YOUR RETIREMENT ACCOUNT YOUR NUMBER-ONE FINANCIAL PRIORITY. THIS IS YOUR #1 JOB.** Again, financing is available for college and most major expenditures, but financing is **NOT** available for retirement. Moreover, the needed retirement fund is much larger than the amount needed to fund all or a portion of a child's advanced education.

The initial requirement is to clarify the difference between saving and investing. Saving is simply income not spent and can include both deferring consumption and reducing recurring costs. Putting money aside for your future is an example. Savings should be held in a safe, an insured account like a bank, or a money market account that does not have a risk of declining value. The act of saving is the first step in creating a pool of funds to be invested. Savings should be without risks.

Investing is spending money from the savings pool with the expectation of achieving a profit or higher return on your money. Investing involves taking risks to improve on the rate of return. Sometimes the terms *saving* and *investing* are used interchangeably, but you need to understand the differences.

Saving can be as easy as starting with an attitude adjustment. Saving money begins with a positive mindset that says you WANT to save because you know you NEED to save.

Recent research has indicated that approximately 50% of Americans own stock through a 401(k), IRA, other retirement accounts, and directly in personal investment portfolios. This group represents a growing investor class in our country. The actual percentage of people owning stock may be even higher, as many investors have entered the market for the first time during the pandemic.

Since 1975, investors have increasingly embraced new paradigms and rules for investing. The nation's process for investing has been divided between active and passive money management.

Active money management is considered a more hands-on activity, entailing selection of individual stocks and bonds and employing other trading strategies in the hope of outperforming particular benchmarks. Only a few money managers consistently do better than passive funds. One of the world's most famous active investors is Warren Buffett.

The late John Bogle, CEO of the Vanguard Group at the time, created the first index fund, a form of passive investing with low costs and low trading activity. Passive investing hopes to match the performance of selected benchmarks. Passive investments usually involve using mutual funds, ETFs, and index funds.

Today passive investing controls approximately 50% of the total stock market value. The performance results of passive investing usually work best for the majority of investors.

The world's largest sovereign-wealth fund is a bastion of passive investing. Norway's Oil Fund, managed by CEO Nicolai Tangen, uses an allocation of 70% stocks mostly passively managed and 30% other investments with an overall estimated value of $1.265 trillion. Norway's sovereign-wealth fund offers strong evidence of the value of passive investing.

To some people, "wealth" is a dirty word—or at least a word often mumbled under the breath as a slur. But if you ask ordinary citizens NOT about their *wealth* but about their *savings* in retirement accounts, many can tell you those values to the nearest one-hundred dollars. We need to think of "wealth-building" for retirement as another phrase for saving. If we do, the savings rate may improve without any sense of guilt or negative social implications. We need to understand that saving is a politically correct concept!

Anecdotal stories about draconian methods to save money that take the fun out of life are readily available. Changes in your spending habits do not need to be dramatic to effectively save money. Here are a few ideas on ways to save money without totally changing your lifestyle:

- Saving for an emergency fund is a start. Begin with small amounts and increase them over time.
- Saving automatically can take the work out of the saving process. Establish an automatic monthly transfer from a checking account to a savings account and watch the savings balance grow. It's harder to spend the money when it is out of the checking account.
- Save windfalls like an inheritance, work bonus, or tax refund.
- Take advantage of any employer match in a 401(k) account by contributing at least an amount equal to the match.
- Save coins and one-dollar bills from everyday change.

- Unsubscribe from marketing emails from retail stores to remove the temptation to buy merchandise. Unsubscribe from publications and read the same information online.
- Drop the landline and rely on your cell phone.
- Pay off high-interest-rate credit cards and avoid credit card debt going forward. Learn to live within the amount of money earned monthly. This is living within your means.
- Put bills on auto-pay and avoid any late fees.
- Designate one day a week as a "no-spend" day.
- Brown-bag your lunch; prepare meals at home; drink water when out for a meal and avoid soft drinks, tea, and coffee, which add extra costs.
- Reduce utility costs by turning off lights when not in use, lower the heating, and raise the AC temperature settings.
- Lower the temperature on the hot water heater to 120 degrees.
- Become a coupon user in shopping for everyday items. Shop by your grocery list and stay focused on it while at the store. Impulse buying can be expensive.
- Research for a cheaper cell phone plan, lower-cost Internet provider, and lower cable TV expenses. Do you need cable TV? Cut the cord!
- Do you really use or need that gym membership? Work out at home and in the park, and use the nature trails for walking that are available to all.
- Ask about discounts available at stores, motels, restaurants, and movie theaters for seniors, students, teachers, AAA members, or veterans. Sometimes offering to pay cash may save you a small percentage off the purchase price. Take advantage of discounts.

You get the idea about the many ways to save money. Making these types of minor changes in your daily routine will not affect your lifestyle. However, they will noticeably increase your source of funds for savings.

Investing, on the other hand, can be a complex subject, and I want to simplify the topic so it is easier for you to begin this journey. It is essential to begin investing early (at a young age) because the power of investing can be magnified over time. This concept is called the power of compound interest. The longer you invest, the more potential success you can achieve.

Every investment carries a risk. This is the first big difference between saving and investing. When you start investing, think about the big picture. If you are buying common stocks, mutual funds, or exchange-traded funds (ETFs), you are buying an ownership position in specific companies. If you are buying real estate, you are taking on property ownership and all that goes with it.

Be realistic about expected rates of return. Historically, the stock market has averaged a 10% return, as reported for the S&P 500. Year-to-year returns can be volatile and may not approach this average in any one year. I recommend using a lower, more conservative expected return of 6% to estimate your future investment growth.

Owning real estate directly can produce an 8–10% annual return. This is considered a good return. Investing in real estate can add diversification to your portfolio. Not all investors want to be a landlord with midnight calls about the toilet overflowing. For those wanting to own real estate like a common stock, it can be as easy as buying a mutual fund or real estate investment trust (REIT). This is a passive way to own real estate assets.

Successful investing requires a long-term perspective. I recommend the buy-and-hold approach to stock market investing. This means you typically hold an investment for five years or longer, unless something dramatic happens to the companies in which you have invested. You only achieve the average returns in a buy-and-hold approach.

If you time the market and jump in and out of investments, there are no average returns to measure against. Market timing is closely related to day trading. Day trading is the speculative buying and selling of securities on the same day, often online, on the basis of small, short-term price fluctuations. Many new-to-the-market stock traders try this approach until they suffer significant dollar losses. These newbie traders are not investing; they are gambling, and they can easily become compulsive gamblers over time. I do not recommend day trading as a strategy.

A third category of investing includes buying bonds: either individual bonds or multiple bonds as part of a pool within a bond fund. Companies and governments finance themselves by issuing bonds with various interest rates and different maturities. Three of the most common types of bonds are corporate, municipal, and government bonds. These are all debt instruments used to raise capital.

When you buy a bond or bond fund, you become a lender, as you are loaning money to the issuer of that bond. In exchange, you will receive interest payments on a specified basis, usually semi-annually, until the bond matures. At maturity, the face amount of the bond is repaid.

Bonds are considered a lower risk for investors than stocks, but certainly not risk-free. Bond defaults make the headlines with growing frequency. The best indicators of bond risks are the ratings of the bonds by one of three rating agencies: Standard & Poor's, Moody's, and Fitch. These ratings rank the bonds from best quality to poorest quality with the following using Standard & Poor's system: AAA, AA, A, BBB+, BBB, BBB-, and so on, through D. The higher the rating, the lower the risk and the lower the expected return. Investors typically group bond ratings into two categories: investment grade and high-yield or junk bonds. Bonds rated below BBB- are known as junk bonds. If you want to invest in bonds, I recommend you stay with investment-grade bonds rated BBB- or better.

One of the biggest misconceptions about investing is that it is reserved for the rich or is only for those who can afford to lose their investments. This is not true with today's commission-free online trading accounts. You can start small and increase your investments as you gain confidence. Start with opening an online investment account with professional money managers such as Vanguard, Schwab, Fidelity, or TD Ameritrade. Alternatively, hire a financial advisor.

To oversimplify the process of starting to invest, here are some of the best investment ideas for beginning everyday investors.

- Participate in your employer-sponsored 401(k) retirement plan.
- Open an IRA or Roth IRA and invest online.
- Automate monthly contributions to these tax-advantaged funds.
- Contact one of the professional money managers listed above and inquire about their robo-advisors.
- From those same professional money advisors, consider their target-date mutual funds.
- Purchase index funds tracking broad market indexes like the S&P 500 index fund (SPY) or Vanguard Total Stock Market Index Fund (VTI).

- Invest in exchange-traded funds (ETFs) with lower expense ratios.
- Buy fractional shares of companies to acquire a small piece of the broader market.
- Research investment apps for beginning investors like Acorns, Stash, Robinhood, or Betterment.

There are many easy-to-use tools to help you ease into investment with small amounts of cash. If you lack the self-confidence to invest on your own, I recommend you hire a financial advisor to help you build a retirement portfolio that will meet your needs. Some financial advisors may require a minimum of $100,000 in investable funds to work with you as a client. Ask friends or family members for recommendations for advisors in your area or go online to www.NAPFA.org (National Association of Personal Financial Advisors) or the Financial Planning Association (www. PlannerSearch.org) to find the names of financial advisors who may take a more comprehensive approach.

If you can save early, often, and regularly, you will be ahead of many Americans who are living paycheck to paycheck. You can do this!

Sometimes family situations can make it difficult for parents to save while they are spending heavily on child rearing while also saving for future college expenditures. While conventional wisdom calls for saving early, often, and regularly, there are times when this is just not possible. The risk for parents in this situation is that increasing their savings demands adding one more spinning plate when they are already managing several. It may be okay for parents to cut short on retirement saving in these child-rearing years, **IF** they are committed to a catch-up plan later.

This catch-up plan will involve saving more as they transition into becoming "empty nesters." If they are behind in funding their retirement accounts when the children leave home, dedicating a greater share of their income toward retirement savings from that point on can work.

This catch-up strategy may be the most realistic way for many families to deal with the financial pressures of raising and educating children. Rather than assuming it's too late to make a difference in their retirement savings, people in the empty-nester phase should take aggressive action to bridge the gap to a well-funded retirement account.

CHAPTER NINE

RULE #6

OPPORTUNITY COSTS

Rule #6 is all about saving for other asset purchases like an auto, a boat, a camper, a home, or a recreational vehicle (RV). Each of these can be a high-dollar purchase. Trying to pay for such expensive assets from cash flow places too much stress on your current earnings. Rule #6 is about understanding opportunity costs to aid in your financial decision-making about how to approach these larger-dollar purchases.

A purchase of assets like those listed above may best be handled as a loan, making payments over time while enjoying the use of the acquired purchase. That means rather than saving the entire purchase price, you only need to save for the down payment, which is easier and quicker.

The down-payment approach I have described comes from the economic concept known as "opportunity cost." Opportunity costs exist because the decision to engage in one activity means foregoing some other activity.

With low interest rates available for loans secured by the types of assets listed above, the question of paying cash versus financing the purchase comes into play. In the current low-interest-rate environment, financing is a popular choice.

Opportunity costs are more than a theory; they are a practical reality. When economists refer to "opportunity cost," they are referring to the value lost or foregone on an alternative use of cash versus the current choice of spending that cash. For example, "idle cash balances in a checking account represent an opportunity cost in terms of lost interest earned." A more simple explanation of "opportunity cost" is the cost of a missed opportunity.

Think in terms of "tradeoff" when you hear the phrase "opportunity cost." With every choice you make, there are tradeoffs to consider. Weigh what you are getting against what you are giving up. Tradeoffs can be measured in terms of dollars, time, and enjoyment or satisfaction.

Examples of opportunity cost in daily life can be demonstrated by the cash-versus-financing choice presented at the beginning of this chapter. Other examples might include the following:

- Take a vacation now or save the money and invest in a house later.
- Attend college today in anticipation of generating a higher income in the future, or begin working and don't go to college.
- Pay down debt now or use the money to generate additional profits over time.

Considering the impact of opportunity costs can guide you in making more profitable decisions. In general, it means having to choose one option over another involving money, time, or lifestyle choices and living with the consequences. When you choose saving over consumption, the opportunity cost is that you will have less money to buy goods and services today. Always look at the cost versus the benefit of each decision. Make sure the tradeoffs are worth it.

Now that you understand the importance of establishing a contingency account (emergency fund); have evaluated paying off a mortgage early or not; provided for educational expenses using tax-deferred qualified tuition plans; mastered saving early, often, and regularly; and implemented the concept of evaluating the opportunity costs of each financial decision, you can dramatically increase your long-term accumulation of funds for retirement. You are now ready to focus on Rule #7, the importance of having multiple sources of income in retirement.

CHAPTER TEN

RULE #7

HAVE MULTIPLE INCOME SOURCES IN RETIREMENT

Rule #7 emphasizes the importance of not depending on a single source of income in retirement. One common goal for retirement plans is to create reliable income to support your lifestyle.

Many people who are retiring find themselves feeling lost when they no longer have a job or career. Their identity has been all about what they *do,* not who they *are.* Without some type of employment, this group is at risk of developing periods of depression and a gradual withdrawal from social interactions.

Working part-time in retirement can be a satisfying use of their time while extending their retirement savings and developing new social contacts. I encourage you to consider some type of part-time work as a way to glide smoothly into full retirement. In today's world, there is so much uncertainty about the future that most people will continue working as long as they can.

A host of benefits from part-time work after reaching full retirement age (FRA) have been documented. The year and month you reach FRA depends on the year you were born. If you were born in 1960 or later, your FRA is age 67.

BENEFITS OF PART-TIME WORK

- A feeling of personal fulfillment and a sense of purpose.
- Financial support that is either needed to live on or provides extra income.
- The opportunity to socialize with other workers, which promotes personal wellbeing.
- The opportunity to explore something new and exciting by learning about new products and services.

What are some part-time jobs that can contribute extra income? The following list is brief, as potential job opportunities depend on your health, previous job experience, and how much time you are willing to commit to part-time work.

EXAMPLES OF PART-TIME WORK

- Doing project work for your previous full-time employer.
- Acting as a consultant with businesses from your contact list.
- Working as a bookkeeper or month-end accountant's assistant.
- Driving for Lyft, Uber, or DoorDash as part of the gig economy.
- Working as a school bus driver, substitute teacher, special education paraprofessional, or online virtual teacher of a specific course.
- Doing call center shift work as a customer service representative.
- Working as a cashier.
- Handling home-based data entry or computer coding.
- Converting a hobby to a money-making business.

- Assisting family members with their entrepreneurial venture.
- Working as a seasonal employee for a government agency, such as the Internal Revenue Service (IRS) during tax season from January to May.

One often overlooked but fulfilling and money-generating opportunity is converting a hobby to a profit-oriented venture. Here are a few examples of ways people have done that.

Some individuals enjoy **woodworking** and furniture restoration. Perhaps it is time for this activity to move out of the garage into a rented space to take on more volume and exposure to the market. What about opening an antique furniture stall at a local flea market?

Copyediting that has been done for a casual purpose or within another job over the years is another example. Book publishers, magazine editors, copyediting companies, writers, and candidates for a master's degree or PhD degree are always looking for a basic spelling, grammar, and punctuation edit of a written work. This can be a part-time endeavor done from home as a freelance service.

If you are talented in **interior design and decorating,** this can be another area to explore for compensation. Working as an independent consultant or joining with an interior design firm for project work can increase your social interactions as well as generate additional income.

If you enjoy **knitting or crocheting**, consider consigning some of your homemade items to retail shops for sale to the general public. Offer to make unique items on a commission basis for customers wanting a college theme, amateur team logos, or a special association insignia.

One positive outcome of the coronavirus pandemic has been the exponential growth in working from home, called remote working. It has received a very positive reception from many employees. Remote working can give you an advantage as you pursue part-time work opportunities. No longer are you limited by geographical distance. Remote work has also shifted many individuals' priorities toward living where they prefer rather than where they work.

Working part-time can affect your Social Security benefits. If you decide to take Social Security benefits prior to achieving FRA, there is a salary cap of $18,950 in 2021. Be careful not to exceed this limit. If you begin Social Security at age 62, your payments are already permanently reduced by 25–30%. If you exceed the salary cap, your benefits will be lowered even more. Any extra income could increase surcharges for Medicare parts B and D as well. If you are at full retirement age (FRA) and over, there is no salary limit.

An often-misunderstood myth about taking Social Security benefits early is that those benefits will be recalculated when you reach FRA. This will not happen! If you choose to take Social Security benefits anytime before FRA, those monthly benefits are forever lower. The only adjustment to these monthly benefits will be the annual cost-of-living (COLA) adjustment applied universally. Consider very carefully whether taking Social Security benefits before FRA is right for you.

The three biggest mistakes people make that will lower their Social Security benefits permanently are:

1. Not working to their full retirement age (FRA); people born in 1955 currently have an FRA of 66 years and 2 months. This FRA gradually increases to age 67 for those born in 1960 or later.

2. Not working at least a full 35 years and contributing to Social Security over that time.
3. Not reviewing their annual Social Security statement and looking for mistakes that should be corrected.

If you are age 70 ½ and start receiving required minimum distributions (RMD) from a traditional rollover IRA or 401(k) plan, these RMD distributions will count as ordinary income, unless they come from a Roth IRA. If you have a Roth IRA, there are no requirements for RMDs. You can withdraw funds from a Roth without penalty or taxes anytime after you reach age 59 ½ if the account is at least five years old.

Going forward, RMDs will begin at age 72 for traditional IRAs. The Secure Act pushes the age that triggers RMDs from 70 ½ to 72, which means you can let your retirement funds grow for an extra 1 ½ years before tapping into them for RMDs. This delay may boost your overall retirement savings. These new rules apply to those who turn 70 ½ in 2020 or later.

President Franklin D. Roosevelt signed the Social Security Act into law on August 14, 1935. In addition to several provisions for general welfare, the new act created a social insurance program designed to pay retired workers age 65 or older a continuing income after retirement.

These benefits are more modest than many realize. For someone who worked all of their adult life at an average salary and retires at age 65, Social Security benefits will replace only about 40% of past earnings. This safety net is available to almost all working adults reaching retirement age.

More than half of all retired Americans rely on Social Security benefits for at least half of their income, although Social Security was never intended to be the primary financial resource to support individuals in retirement. When discussing the background of the Social Security system, Dwight D. Eisenhower had this to say: "The system is not intended as a substitute for private savings, pension plans and insurance protection. It is, rather, intended as the foundation upon which these other forms of protection can be soundly built. Thus, the individual's own work, his planning and his thrift will bring him a higher standard of living upon his retirement, or his family a higher standard of living in the event of his death, than would otherwise be the case. Hence the system both encourages thrift and self-reliance and helps to prevent destitution in our national life."

Social Security benefits are the primary source of income for many retirees. Use the online tool offered by the Social Security Administration to help estimate your future benefits. Go online to www.SSA.gov/benefitcalculators. AARP also has good information about maximizing these benefits. Go online to www.AARP.org and follow the tab to the Social Security calculator.

Some forms of Social Security benefits are available between the ages of 62–70. You must claim these benefits no later than age 70. The longer you wait to claim Social Security, the more your benefit amount can increase. Typically, each year you delay claiming Social Security past FRA, your payout increases by 8%.

POTENTIAL INCOME SOURCES

- Social Security benefits
- Part-time employment
- Self-employment in a new venture
- Investment income
- Pension payments

- Fixed annuities
- Bank certificates of deposit
- RMD distributions
- Real estate rental income
- Online sales income from selling on Craigslist, eBay, Instagram, Etsy, Marketplace, and other platforms

Working part-time in retirement clearly has a number of benefits. However, there are potential downsides to consider as well. My advice is to make an informed decision on part-time employment as an additional income source.

I have heard some people remark that we need to "retire retirement," a phrase coined by Ken Dychtwald, CEO of Age Wave, and adapted from a Harvard Business School book titled *Workforce Crisis*. This concept reflects the need and desire for older workers to work part-time in retirement. It emerged due to the serious problem of a shrinking workforce. The problem is clear. As our economy nears full employment, finding workers will remain a difficult problem in many sectors of the economy. A shrinking workforce can pose a demographic threat to our nation's future job growth and overall productivity.

It starts with a shortage of talented workers. The general population is aging, people are living longer and healthier lifestyles, and the birth rate in the U.S. has reached an historic low. These factors cause the labor market to tighten.

All of a sudden, older employees have more choices about where, when, and how they work. The most skilled, talented, and capable among this group are likely to be mobile and financially independent. The challenge for employers is to find new ways to reconnect with employees before they retire and run to a competitor to work on their own terms. The answer:

Retire retirement and learn to attract and retain older workers by offering flexible hours, part-time pay, partial benefits, and generous policies for time off. Through such arrangements, the *retire retirement* concept can be a win-win for employers and employees.

Building a well-funded retirement plan involves accessing a variety of income-producing assets. While investing in stocks and bonds is an obvious choice, the field of other income-producing investments is broad and varied. Here are examples of other income-producing investments, each with a different risk profile and degree of liquidity.

EXAMPLES OF INCOME-PRODUCING INVESTMENTS

- Investment property – One example is buying a rental property. This investment can produce healthy returns but has limited liquidity, and managing the property can be troublesome and time-consuming.
- Shares in real estate investment trusts (REITs) – This is a form of real estate investing without the need for your direct management. Shares of REITs are sold like stocks. Liquidity is high with the publicly traded REITs.
- Farmland – Over time, farmland has been a good inflation hedge. This investment offers lower liquidity and, if you do not farm the property yourself, can involve higher expenses for sharecropping or negotiating cash rent arrangements. Returns fluctuate with the weather and commodity markets unless you operate on a cash rent basis.
- Peer-to-peer (P2P) lending –First of all, you must live in a state that allows this type of activity. Essentially, this is a form of crowd lending using a website. As a lender, you are investing in a portion of loans being made to borrowers

selected by the website. This can be a form of passive income. The P2P marketplace Prosper (www.Prosper.com) offers an automated investing feature that matches your amount of money being loaned with your set of criteria for borrowers. You may also engage in direct lending to small businesses and their owners. This requires more hands-on management and a background in finance. Risk of non-payment can be a turnoff for many investors. Direct lending may involve expenses for professional services like accounting, legal, and documentation services. Lack of liquidity can be an issue.

- Technology stocks – Technology stocks have been one of the highest-performing sectors this past year. The technology sector has driven much of the stock market's rebound since the low point in March 2020. This performance has generated a lot of interest in U.S. technology companies that have continued to demonstrate rapid growth. If you are interested in investing in technology companies, I recommend looking at a technology sector index fund rather than individual companies. I call this a basket approach to investing. This is when you buy a number of companies pooled together in a basket rather than a single one. Sector investing allows you to make these investments while reducing single-stock risk. In this space, I like the SPDR Technology Select Sector Fund (XLK).

This sector fund offers both income and potentially sizable capital gains or losses. A word of caution: This fund is non-diversified, in that it only invests in technology companies.

SPDR TECHNOLOGY SELECT SECTOR FUND (XLK)
Expense Ratio: 0.13%
Yield: 1.08%

Top holdings include Microsoft, Apple, Visa, MasterCard, Intel Corp, Adobe, Cisco Systems, and other technology companies.

Precious metals investing has received a lot of promotion as a method of hedging against the stock market. I am not a fan of this type of commodity investing. Gold, silver, copper, and other precious metals can offer diversification and an inflation hedge. However, they offer ZERO income. These types of investments require knowledge of commodity markets. While these investments do not pay interest or dividends, they are situated in a more volatile part of the market that can produce good returns when the assets are sold. Precious metals investing can also generate losses of principal. Investing in these assets involves hidden expenses such as fees for storage if purchasing any metals to be stored in physical form, capital gains taxes, and risk of loss, in addition to gaining no monthly income. Unless you are a gambler or have specific expertise, I would stay away from investing in precious metals.

Retirees need to think outside the box about income! Why is it important to have more than one source of income in retirement? A diversified variety of income sources will protect you in the event that a primary income source loses value or becomes unstable. When you were working full-time, you had one primary income source: your paycheck. In retirement, you will need multiple smaller-dollar income sources to continue to support your lifestyle. This is the classic rope, belt, and suspenders approach to generating income in retirement.

You have spent your entire adult life working, spending the money you have earned and, hopefully, saving for retirement. When you are ready to retire, the focus changes from accumulation of assets to creating predictable retirement income out of what you have in your retirement account. It seems everything has been turned upside down. To make this transition, talk with your financial advisor about tailoring a retirement income plan to match your risk tolerance with the amount of income you need to support your lifestyle in retirement.

Now that you understand my Rules of Engagement, it is time to turn your focus to building a personal pension plan.

PART THREE

ENJOY YOUR PENSION

CHAPTER ELEVEN

BUILD A PERSONAL PENSION

Some people are so fixated on wanting a pension that they call it the Holy Grail of retirement. Most retirees want and need predictable lifetime income. After all, longevity has real consequences like running out of money if one does not plan well.

Building a personal pension should not be so difficult that everyday investors would have trouble accomplishing this financial task. There are a number of ways to create a monthly income similar to what a company pension typically provides.

CREATE YOUR OWN PENSION

- Delay filing for Social Security benefits until FRA, or wait until age 70, if you can.
- Purchase an immediate, fixed annuity and receive a monthly income for life. Go to www.ImmediateAnnuities.com and compare various annuity contracts and payouts. Age is a factor for the payout percentages. Talk with your insurance agent about your options.
- Build a diversified portfolio and set up monthly withdrawals with a check-a-month plan.
- Build a portfolio with dividends and interest payments flowing regularly from these investments. Live off the cash flow.

- Build a rollover IRA and live off of required minimum distributions (RMDs) monthly.
- Use any windfall like an inheritance, an unexpected lump sum buyout from work, an all-cash acquisition of one of your investments, or any other liquidity event to fund a personal pension.

Building a personal pension should not depend on one individual financial product. The most successful pension plans incorporate a multiplicity of financial products. Combining Social Security benefits with an immediate, fixed annuity could provide enough money to cover most of your living expenses. Adding one or two of the other pension-like options such as a rollover IRA or a diversified portfolio for monthly income withdrawals completes the pension package.

Building a personal pension plan is similar to building a house. You must complete numerous stages of construction in the proper order to obtain a finished product you can be proud of.

CONSTRUCTION OF A PENSION PLAN

HOUSE CONSTRUCTION	PENSION PLAN CONSTRUCTION
1. Design a house plan.	1. Commit to building a personal pension plan.
2. Buy a building lot.	2. Set a goal: Determine how much income will be needed in retirement.
3. Complete foundation.	3. Begin saving, building an emergency fund and funding an IRA and 401(k) account.
4. Build the frame and roof.	4. Invest by choosing index funds, ETFs, and mutual funds with low costs.

5. Paint, decorate, and landscape.	5. Adjust asset allocations by your age, maintain broad diversification, keep investment costs low, and stay focused on the long-term goal.
6. Move in.	6. Enjoy the good life of a well-funded pension plan.

Yes, you can still have a pension by designing it yourself (DIY) or working with a financial advisor to create one. Through either a DIY approach or by working with a financial advisor, you can satisfy the pension envy that many retirees experience as they seek financial security in retirement. Chapter Twelve will present a detailed blueprint for the construction of a personal pension.

In general terms, here is an outline of the financial decisions and actions involved in building a personal pension. Keep in mind that younger investors can take more risks, while investors closer to retirement need to be more conservative.

CONSIDERATIONS FOR CREATING A PENSION PLAN

- Think about your retirement goals and how long you have before you retire. Have a firm number of years in mind before retirement.
- Estimate how much money you will need in retirement. Use an online calculator.
- Implement a savings program. Automate this plan for simplicity.
- Launch an investment program. Understand your risk tolerance.
- Establish an IRA or a Roth IRA.
- Participate in any company-sponsored 401(k) plan or other retirement savings plan.

- Refresh the plans to keep them current. Retirement plans evolve through the years, so rebalancing choices and life changes may affect your plans. Consolidate into a rollover IRA as you change jobs, for instance.
- If you doubt your ability to design a plan on your own, engage a professional financial advisor to guide you to your goals. Keep your eyes on the end goal and the options it will provide.

Start planning for retirement as soon as you can to take advantage of the power of compounding each year's growth. "A goal without a plan is just a wish," says French author Antoine de Saint-Exupéry. Planning should be immediately followed by taking action to implement your plan. The biggest hurdle in building a pension or retirement plan is getting started!

Broadly speaking, the key risks that should be addressed in any retirement plan are as follows:

1. Longevity risks – Outliving your money by living longer than the average expected lifespan.
2. Stock market volatility – Retiring during a highly volatile time in the market, or needing money when the market has taken a nose-dive.
3. Inflation – While inflation has been low for the past few years, there have been times in the past when inflation grew more rapidly than market returns.
4. Healthcare and long-term care – Costs in both areas continue to increase, and planning for the rising cost of healthcare is important.
5. Focus on living – Retirement is about more than sitting in a rocking chair and drinking coffee; it is about enjoying life with a purpose.

6. Legacy – Plan carefully how you want to be remembered both with shared memories and physical gifts you want to leave to your heirs.

BUILDING A PENSION WHILE SELF-EMPLOYED

If you are self-employed and do not have access to a company-sponsored 401(k) plan, there are a number of tax-advantaged products available from which you can build a retirement plan. This is a do-it-yourself project.

- Traditional IRA/Roth IRA – This has the same annual limits and catch-up provisions for self-employed individuals as for anyone with an earned income. Contribution limits in 2021 are the lesser of earned income or $6,000 with a catch up of $1,000 for those age 50 or older. Up to $6,000 can also be contributed for a nonworking spouse.
- Solo 401(k) – This product is for a business owner without employees other than a spouse. Contribution limits in 2021 are $58,000 plus a catch up of $6,500 or 100% of earned income, whichever is less.
- Sep IRA – The Sep IRA is best suited for self-employed people with only a few employees. Contribution limits in 2021 are $58,000 or up to 25% of compensation. Employers must contribute an equal percentage of salary for each eligible employee. The amount to be contributed is flexible and can change from year to year, based on the profitability of the company. Employees CANNOT contribute to these plans.
- Simple IRA – This product is designed for larger employers with up to 100 employees. Contribution limits in 2021 are $13,500 plus a catch up of $3,000.

If these products are of interest, I suggest you research the details of each one before making a decision. Working with a financial advisor as a self-employed business owner, contractor or gig worker can help you select the best product for your employment situation.

Do not become so focused on any one financial component of a retirement plan that you overlook the value of one of the best annuities available: Social Security. The longer you wait to begin drawing benefits under Social Security, the larger the monthly payout for the rest of your life. The time to begin to draw Social Security benefits expires at age 70. These benefits can be part of the foundation of your personal cash flow plan in retirement.

SIMPLE PENSION PLAN

If you want a pension-like plan for monthly income in retirement, here's how to create one. I call this my SIMPLE PENSION PLAN.

The components of my Simple Pension Plan involve only two income sources: Social Security benefits and required minimum distributions (RMD) from a rollover IRA. It is important to refrain from drawing on these funds until age 70 and 70 ½, respectively. This will maximize the benefits of both.

The formula for my Simple Pension Plan can be expressed as follows:

SOCIAL SECURITY + RMD = SIMPLE PENSION PLAN

For this pension plan to work best, it is necessary to fund an IRA for as many years as possible. I recommend depositing the maximum allowed funds annually (currently $6,000 + $1,000 catch up after age 50) and transferring any company 401(k) account balances into a master rollover IRA. Transfer the 401(k) accounts when you leave one employer for another and when you retire from your last job.

With all IRA and 401(k) balances combined in a rollover IRA, establish monthly payments with your RMD at age 70 ½. Waiting until age 70 to draw on your Social Security benefits will maximize these monthly payments for the rest of your life.

My Simple Pension Plan may provide enough monthly income to meet your living expenses. If it doesn't, you will need to graduate to a more robust pension plan, as outlined in the next chapter.

The key to this Simple Pension Plan is to start funding an IRA as soon as you have earned income and maximize the funding every year. Adding a company-sponsored 401(k) account to this formula will give you additional money in retirement.

Everyday investors should realize there is no perfect strategy to replace a monthly income after you leave the workforce. Each individual and family has different needs. However, it is possible with good retirement planning to have a high level of confidence that you will not outlive your money.

CHAPTER TWELVE

RETIRE WITH MORE, NOT LESS—PART I

You are not alone if you are worried about having enough income to replace your steady paycheck in retirement. More than 23% of workers are not confident they will have enough money to live on in retirement, according to a 2019 Retirement Confidence Survey. This same survey also noted that 40% of workers have saved less than $25,000 for retirement. Now you see why I believe the U.S. is facing a retirement crisis.

When I talk with people who feel worried about having enough money in retirement, I ask a basic question: "How much money is enough?" You should see their puzzled look as they try to come up with a dollar amount to answer my question. What I am seeking is not a dollar amount but an indication of the lifestyle they want in retirement.

By the time adults reach retirement age, they have established spending patterns and a lifestyle they have crafted over time. Unless they plan to change their lifestyle dramatically in retirement, they know what amount of money it takes to support their current comfort level. Replacing at least 85% of your existing income is a beginning point to calculate how much money will be needed in retirement.

Some pundits say the answer to how much is enough is $1 more than is needed. John D. Rockefeller's answer was "Just a little bit more." The answer for most retiring couples can be very simply, "Enough to do what we want to do when we want to do it!" If this is an answer fitting your lifestyle, then you will have something that is very elusive to many. You will be able to say, "I have something most people will never have—I have enough."

I do not want to make light of the importance of determining how much money you will need in retirement. This is one of the first steps in developing a retirement plan. Here are some rules of thumb that have worked for years in estimating the amount of money needed for your retirement. These rules of thumb are good for estimating only, as our lives are constantly changing.

RULE-OF-THUMB OPTIONS

- Here is a broad rule of thumb: Multiply your current annual spending by 25. The answer is the size of retirement portfolio you will need to conservatively withdraw 4% every year to live on. For example, if you are currently spending $40,000 a year in expenses, 25 times that number is $1,000,000. This rule of thumb works best when you are around age 50 or more. Younger workers may be in lower-paid jobs, so their spending is reduced to match that level of income and, therefore, not a good predictor of their retirement fund requirements.
- Here is more background on the 4% rule. This popular withdrawal strategy was presented by Bill Bengen, a financial advisor, in a 1994 article in the *Journal of Financial Planning*. It has been debated and dissected by experts ever since, with many characterizing it as overly simplistic. The rule works like this: Withdraw no more than 4% of your retirement savings in the first year and then adjust for inflation in the years following. Recently, Bengen revised his rule to allow for withdrawing 4.5–5.0%. While the

4% rule of thumb has historically worked, using it today with the current low bond returns seems problematic. Some academics recommend lowering the rule to 3.5% because of the low-interest-rate environment. The point is, investors can only survive by making adjustments to their withdrawal rate based on changing circumstances. The key is to use any withdrawal rate rule of thumb as a *guideline*, **NOT** a written-in-stone rule. The only safe withdrawal rate is a flexible one.

- Another rule of thumb is called the *income replacement approach*. If you currently earn $100,000 a year, your goal should be to replace 75–85% of your pre-retirement income. On average, people in the U.S. live at least 20 years after retirement. In this example, replacing 85% of your pre-retirement income would look like this: 100,000 x 85% = 85,000 x 20 years = $1,700,000. This approach does not work well for younger workers.

- Use a retirement calculator to estimate how much money you need in retirement based on age and income. There are many calculators to choose from. Look at websites sponsored by Fidelity, Schwab, Vanguard, or TD Ameritrade and follow their instructions. These calculators give you another example of an estimate based on funds needed in retirement.

- I like using the retirement calculator from AARP. Go to www.AARP.org and look for retirement calculators. This calculator can help you estimate the retirement nest egg you need for a secure retirement. It is interactive and uses your personal data to customize this estimate.

Let me repeat this key piece to solving the retirement puzzle. One of the biggest takeaways of this exercise should be the fact that the number derived is just an estimate. It is based on many assumptions, so just use any of these methodologies as a guideline to establish a financial goal.

In the previous chapter, I outlined my Simple Pension Plan. If you need more monthly income than the Simple Pension Plan generates, you may need a more robust pension plan with at least two or three more components in addition to the Simple Pension Plan.

ROBUST PENSION PLAN

My formula for a more robust pension plan providing additional monthly income is as follows:

SIMPLE PENSION PLAN + INVESTMENT PORTFOLIO FOR INCOME + A FIXED ANNUITY + CASH OR OTHER LIQUID ASSETS = ROBUST PENSION PLAN

If you want a more robust pension like monthly income in retirement, here is how to get started designing it yourself. People seem to like the security of monthly checks. In designing a personal pension, it is important to remember that income is part of your retirement strategy rather than the *only* strategy. A healthy and sustainable robust retirement plan has at least six components.

A HEALTHY RETIREMENT PLAN

1. Cash or other liquid assets
2. Social Security benefits
3. A pension for income: either a corporate plan, a fixed annuity, or a personal pension
4. A 401(k) fully funded account for growth

5. An IRA/Roth IRA fully funded for growth
6. Other investments for growth and income

For a more robust pension plan, I have combined all of the elements of a retirement plan that can generate income. Some growth is still possible from an investment portfolio with growth stocks that also generate some income. My robust pension plan maximizes income.

With these components, you can have a stable income and total financial flexibility to adapt to changes in retirement living. These components are interconnected, and the plan works best when they are operating in harmony.

GRAPHIC COMPONENTS OF A RETIREMENT PLAN

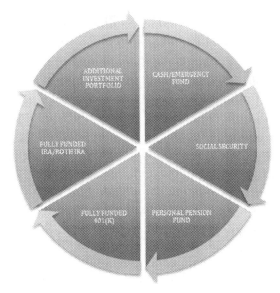

As discussed in Chapter Eleven, building a retirement plan involves combining several income sources. These varied income sources can provide a more reliable income stream. At least four inputs are involved in building out the details in this approach, in addition to part-time employment.

RETIREMENT INCOME SOURCES

- Social Security benefits
- Immediate or fixed annuities; some form of a pension plan
- Investment portfolio of income-producing stocks and bonds
- Rollover IRA/401(k)

A retirement plan starts with Social Security. Most working adults qualify for Social Security benefits by the time they reach age 62. Other types of Social Security payments that are available include Supplemental Security Income (SSI), disability payments, survivors' benefits, and retirement benefits. We are focused only on retirement benefits here.

I recommend delaying taking Social Security benefits for as long as you can, if you are healthy and continue to work. You must begin receiving your benefits no later than age 70. The full retirement age (FRA) has increased from age 65 to age 67. If you were born between 1943 and 1954, your full retirement age is 66. If you were born in 1960 or later, your full retirement age is 67. Go to www. SSA.gov to find your FRA using their retirement age calculator.

A few categories of American workers will NOT qualify for Social Security retirement benefits. This situation is relatively rare. Here is a short list of some of those who are excluded from Social Security retirement benefits:

1. THOSE WITHOUT ENOUGH SOCIAL SECURITY CREDITS – A minimum requirement to collect Social

Security retirement benefits is 40 work credits, or approximately 10 years of work while paying into the Social Security system.

2. WORKERS WHO DIE BEFORE AGE 62 – Age 62 is the minimum age to begin collecting Social Security retirement benefits.

3. CERTAIN DIVORCED SPOUSES – If a marriage lasted fewer than 10 years, the spouse is not eligible to claim benefits from their former spouse's earnings record.

4. WORKERS WHO RETIRE IN CERTAIN FOREIGN COUNTRIES – There is a short list of countries where the U.S. government will not send Social Security payments. One example is North Korea. You can check the entire list on the Social Security website.

5. CERTAIN GOVERNMENT EMPLOYEES – If these workers did not pay Social Security taxes, they are not eligible to receive these retirement benefits.

6. CERTAIN IMMIGRANTS OVER THE AGE OF 65 – Retired people who immigrate to the U.S. will not have the 40 minimum work credits.

Buying a fixed or immediate annuity is one way to obtain monthly income for life. Annuities are insurance contracts. When you purchase a fixed annuity, you have effectively eliminated two significant risks: stock market risk and longevity risk. Longevity risk is the possibility that you will live so long you run out of money. With a fixed annuity, you will receive a monthly check for life.

On the surface, fixed annuities sound too good to be true, and like all financial products, there are downsides to consider. First, they require an upfront lump-sum payment. This can be a sizable amount, and it is non-refundable. You cannot access this cash payment for any reason going forward.

Second, the monthly payouts will remain the same for the rest of your life. Fixed annuities do not provide any protection for inflation and the rising cost of living, unless you purchase an expensive inflation rider.

Third, you assume some credit risk with the choice of an insurance provider. There are ways to mitigate this risk, but it requires more homework on your part.

Finally, if you die prematurely, typically there are no refunds on a fixed annuity contract. If you die early, the insurance company wins and your estate loses!

There can be beneficiary designations IF you pay extra for this option. With a fixed annuity, the beneficiary receives the remaining present value of payments. If you purchase a refund option or period certain rider, a beneficiary can receive any remaining payments under the contract.

I am not a big fan of using immediate, fixed annuities for the reasons spelled out above. The loss of financial flexibility by locking in your money and the upfront lump-sum payment lead me to prefer alternative options. Additionally, annuity returns are typically below the long-term S&P 500 Index combined with high fees plus tax issues. This makes me hesitant about recommending annuities.

Perhaps I have a serious case of annuities aversion. But fixed annuities, used properly, have provided benefits to retirees by giving them a lifetime income stream and peace of mind about not outliving their money. Fixed annuities can be a useful way to deal with the challenges of providing monthly income for life. Of all the varieties of annuities, I like the fixed annuity the best. It is a plain vanilla product. You give the insurance company the money, and they pay you a lifetime income. The opportunity cost with this product is the loss of financial flexibility along with a lack of any growth potential. Your specific life circumstances will guide you on whether immediate, fixed annuities are the best option for you.

A combination of Social Security benefits and a steady monthly check from an annuity-like source can meet some retirees' income needs in full retirement. Let me show you how to build an investment portfolio that will contribute to this process.

Here are four different ways I have seen people build their own pension. Each of them has investment risks and requires financial perseverance to achieve success. I will only cover the basics of each approach, as implementation of each method involves myriad details.

PENSION PLAN METHODOLOGIES

1. Immediate, fixed annuity
2. Long-term investing to build an income plan, creating a check-a-month plan
3. Home equity line of credit (HELOC)
4. Inheritance or other lump-sum cash receipts

In each method, it is best to start with a lump sum to achieve faster growth. Having a lump sum as a beginning balance provides for faster compounding to achieve your ultimate savings goal. Number 2 above is the exception, as it is an accumulative process of periodic investments over time.

IMMEDIATE, FIXED ANNUITY – We have already discussed how immediate, fixed annuities work. In this example, you invest a lump sum to purchase an annuity. According to www.Bankrate.

com, these are the expected monthly payouts from a $300,000 investment at 5.0%, with a length of annuity varying from 10–30 years.

30 years: $1,603.78
20 years: $1,971.65
10 years: $3,168.75

INVESTING TO BUILD AN INCOME PLAN – Consistent investing over a long period of time can be an effective method of accumulating a retirement fund. Compound interest makes this a worthwhile strategy. Ultimately, you can use this portfolio for creating a check-a-month plan. This strategy can be more tax-efficient than an immediate annuity, and less costly.

Using this method involves a longer-term approach to investing. It starts with maximizing your annual contributions to an individual IRA/Roth IRA. Currently this amount is $6,000 per year, with an additional $1,000 catch-up for those age 50 or older. Likewise, maximizing any 401(k) account is a requirement. Maximum contributions are currently $19,500 per year, with a $6,500 catch up for those age 50 or older.

Roth IRAs have many advantages. While you cannot deduct contributions to a Roth IRA, qualified distributions are tax-free. You can continue to make contributions to a Roth after age 70 ½, and you can leave balances in a Roth for as long as you are living. There are no RMDs for a Roth IRA. Spousal Roth IRAs are also permitted.

At any time, you may withdraw contributions from a Roth IRA, both tax- and penalty-free. However, there are restrictions when it comes to withdrawing account earnings. Check with your financial advisor for the details of these restrictions.

After maximizing annual contributions to an IRA/Roth IRA and a 401(k) account, additional investments are needed to reach a comfortable retirement goal. If you can average investing an additional $500 per month, you are on your way to achieving financial security in retirement. Look for sources of funds to invest, such as any bonus received, gift money, unused vacation or sick leave pay, tax refunds, and maybe one-half of any second income. Any windfall can be a source of these additional investment dollars.

HOME EQUITY LINE OF CREDIT (HELOC) – Sometime just coming up with a lump sum to jump-start a retirement account can prove challenging. If you have equity in your home, consider taking out a HELOC from your bank. Pay off all high-interest-rate credit cards with the HELOC, and going forward, refrain from charging more than you can pay off each month. Use the balance of the HELOC for investment. This could provide a sum of money to bolster your retirement account while repaying the HELOC over a 10-year period. According to the website NerdWallet, if at age 50 you took out a HELOC and invested it at 7.0%, here are the ending balances of that investment over time:

Amount	Return	15 Years	20 Years	25 Years
$100,000	7.0%	$275,900	$386,900	$542,700
$200,000	7.0%	$551,800	$773,900	$1,085,400

If you assume a full-pay HELOC with a 10-year maturity at 6.0%, the monthly payments to extinguish this debt are manageable.

- A $100,000 HELOC is fully repaid over 10 years with $1,110.21 monthly payments.
- A $200,000 HELOC is fully repaid over 10 years with $2,220.41 monthly payments.

The total principal and interest payments over the life of these HELOC examples are dwarfed by the growth of the retirement fund balances in each of the circumstances shown here. The numbers are even more impressive if the funds are invested for longer than 25 years.

A HELOC is the same as a second mortgage on your home, assuming you have an existing mortgage at the time you initiate a HELOC. If the funds drawn under a HELOC are used for home improvements, and you itemize on your tax return, the IRS allows you to write off interest payments on a HELOC up to a combined first and second mortgage balance of $750,000. If funds from the HELOC are used for other investments, no tax deductions are allowed.

Other than a HELOC, you may qualify for a cash-out refinance on your residence that will provide a lump sum for other investments. Review the costs of each option and make an informed decision.

INHERITANCE – This is the old-fashioned way to build a pension. With an unexpected windfall like a lump sum from an inheritance, rather than spending it, I recommend using some or all of it as the initial deposit to fund a pension. You could buy an immediate, fixed annuity or fund a retirement account focused on income generation in retirement. The expected results could prove similar to the lump sum invested in the HELOC example.

As I have demonstrated, with good planning, you can retire with more than you need to live day to day. By the time you reach full retirement age (FRA), you will be glad you have made these significant long-term choices.

CHAPTER THIRTEEN

RETIRE WITH MORE, NOT LESS—PART II

Building an investment portfolio over time with income-producing stocks and bonds can be a labor of patience and necessity. Patience is said to be a virtue. For many Americans seeking to build financial security in retirement, it can also be an expensive necessity. What I mean is that IF you do not devote time to retirement planning and funding your plan, the result of an underfunded plan will become very expensive. You may run out of money while still living.

IF you do the necessary planning and fund your retirement goals adequately, it is also an expensive necessity. Most retirement goals will require more money than you spent to purchase your home. But it is a necessary expense that will provide a comfortable retirement lifestyle.

While working and saving, the goal of a retirement portfolio is to earn a substantial rate of return without taking undo risks. After retirement, the goal of the portfolio changes from accumulation to income production.

With a retirement portfolio, the need shifts to producing reliable cash flows that will last for the rest of your life. Before focusing on the retirement portfolio, we need to discuss building an investment portfolio while you are still working. I like using a total-return approach in this scenario, as it can provide for a check-a-month solution. I will also discuss the importance of having a draw-down strategy or withdrawal rate during retirement.

With a total-return investment portfolio, select a mix of stock and bond index funds that you think can deliver your expected return over time. As a young investor, you might want to have a higher % of stock than bond funds. This combination will produce more growth in the early years of your investing. An investment mix of 95% stock funds, with no bonds, and 5% cash and/or cash equivalents might be appropriate.

The historical return for the S&P 500 over the past 90 years has been 9.0% plus. The same index average return over the past 20 years has been 7.0% plus. Over the past 10 years, it has produced a 13.6% return. As you can see, the total returns have varied dramatically, depending on the time period. I prefer to use a more conservative expected return of 6.0% in all of my calculations.

As an investor approaches middle age (around age 50), it is appropriate to adjust the risk profile of the portfolio. A mix of 75% stock index funds, 20% bond funds, and 5% cash might be a better allocation. I call this modification process age-risk mitigation.

The five most important factors influencing the performance of an investment portfolio, in my opinion, are asset allocation, diversification, low cost, the passage of time, and investment selection.

SUCCESS FACTORS FOR INVESTMENT PORTFOLIOS

1. Asset allocation
2. Diversification
3. Low costs
4. Time in the market
5. Investment selection

ASSET ALLOCATION – This is nothing more than choosing an asset mix within the portfolio that reflects your financial goals. Another way to describe asset allocation is, "Don't put all your eggs in one basket." Most money managers agree that there are no good or bad allocations, just *your* allocation. With an appropriate asset allocation, you can have more control over the risk level of the portfolio. Different asset classes act in different ways in normal markets.

The typical asset classes are common stocks, bonds, and cash. Sometimes more sophisticated investors include real estate and commodities. Stocks provide an opportunity for growth, while bonds provide stability and income. The core reason for buying bonds hasn't changed. Everyday investors turn to bonds for steady income and capital preservation, as a hedge against volatility in the stock market. Cash is held in reserve to be used for unknown opportunities or emergencies.

In today's low-interest-rate environment, investing in bonds can be challenging. The reality is that age may be less relevant than your circumstances in choosing an asset allocation. If you have a sizable stock portfolio and only draw down small amounts of income annually, you may not need a bond fund. On the other hand, if you need to live off the earnings of your portfolio, you may need bonds for a more stable income, even in a down market.

Ultimately, it really is all about an investor's risk tolerance and ability versus willingness to take on risk. If your risk tolerance is low, you will sleep better at night if you have some mix of bonds in your total portfolio.

DIVERSIFICATION – The second factor is diversification. Think of it this way: Rather than trying to find the needle, buy the entire haystack. This might be called buying the market. The more stocks and bonds you own, the more protection you have against single-issue market losses. This is the essence of what you get when buying a broadly diversified index fund.

Diversification is another word for *spreading the risk*. The S&P 500 index fund (SPY) is more diversified than a portfolio of a few stocks. However, it is not as diversified as a total stock market index fund (VTI).

"Invest in what you know" has long been many everyday investors' philosophy. However, research shows that a smaller portfolio of companies you know and understand is NOT less risky than a diversified portfolio including hundreds or thousands of companies. Most of the returns of the stock market over time are generated by a small number of companies. Your odds of picking these few winners grow stronger by owning an index fund containing all stocks listed on an exchange.

Rather than buying an individual stock you believe will make you wealthy and risking losing everything if you are wrong, you can easily get the diversification you need by buying broad index funds, mutual funds, and exchange-traded funds (ETFs). These financial instruments offer diversification among multiple industries, feature companies of various sizes, and may include hundreds of different companies.

Another way to avoid putting all your money into one stock and hoping for the best is to buy fractional shares. Schwab & Company calls their fractional shares program Schwab Slices. They only allow you to buy fractional shares in the companies included in the S&P 500. Fractional share purchases provide a low-cost method of getting broad market diversification in stocks.

LOW COSTS – The third factor for success is maintaining low costs within your portfolio. It makes sense that the more trading you do, the more costs will increase via transaction fees, capital gains and losses, and taxes. This is one of the reasons I recommend a buy-and-hold strategy. Even with no commissions, with online trading platforms from Fidelity, Schwab, and others, I still follow a buy-and-hold approach.

My answer to keep costs low is to own index funds, also known as passive funds, that track broad markets. In fact, index funds and ETFs combined make a diversified portfolio AND have very low costs or expense ratios.

TIME – Time in the market is superior to market timing when it comes to measuring the total return of an investment portfolio. This is the fourth factor for success. Knowing when to invest is not as important as how long you stay invested. The narrower your investment time horizon, the more vulnerable you are to sudden and unpredictable changes in the market.

Building a comfortable retirement fund balance depends on how much your money grows, but also on how *long* it grows. The single biggest advantage of time in the market is the incredible power of compound interest. Let me show you a simple example of how compound interest works. In the following table, I plot the savings strategies of three fictional individuals. Each of them saved the same amount of money over a 10-year term. They each earned 7% annually on a consistent basis until age 65. The only difference between these investors is the age when they started investing.

POWER OF COMPOUND INTEREST

INVESTOR	AMOUNT INVESTED PER MONTH	AGE INVESTING STARTED	TIME PERIOD SAVED	ENDING BALANCE
A	$1,000	25	10 years	$1,324,426
B	$1,000	35	10 years	$673,271
C	$1,000	45	10 years	$342,257

Investor A saved $1,000 per month starting at age 25 until he turned 35. Then he stopped saving but left his money in his investment account until he retired at age 65.

Investor B didn't start saving until age 35. She saved the same $1,000 per month until she turned 45. She left the balance in her investment account until retirement at age 65.

Investor C was a late bloomer. He didn't start saving until age 45, and he saved the same $1,000 per month for 10 years. At age 55, he stopped saving and left his money in his investment account until his 65th birthday.

Each of these three investors saved the same amount—$120,000—over a 10-year period. Surprisingly, the ending balances in their investment accounts were dramatically different. You can be Investor A if you get started early and let compound interest work for you. If this chart doesn't make you a believer in the power of compound interest, nothing will.

Put time on your side by investing sooner rather than later. The magic of compound interest works every time. Saving a little early always beats saving more later. You will enjoy the combined benefits of compound interest along with time in the market while your portfolio has a chance to grow. Reinvesting dividends through a dividend reinvestment plan (DRIP) and resisting cashing out your investments early are two powerful additional growth factors. Time can have an incredibly important role in supporting a more comfortable lifestyle in the future.

Now you know the four important factors leading to a successful investment portfolio. But what good is this information if you do not know what specific actions are recommended for success? This leads to a fifth factor: making the actual **INVESTMENT SELECTION.**

INVESTMENT SELECTION is the final factor in portfolio success. Remember, you are constructing a portfolio for the long-term, not taking a day-trading position. While there are no universal allocation methodologies that I follow, a modified age allocation may make sense for you. This is another way to manage your individual risk tolerance as you age. I will give you my recommendations for actionable investment portfolio decisions based on very broad age categories in the next few pages.

As important as **rebalancing** is, I do not consider it one of the top five factors in successful investing. Rebalancing is more of a given and occurs when your original asset allocation becomes out of balance. Usually on an annual basis, investors should rebalance their portfolio by realigning the mix of stocks, bonds, and cash to the original allocation mix. This annual activity will help adjust the risk in the portfolio. Sell a portion of the asset class that is overweight and buy a portion of the asset class that is underweight. This process will force you to live by the rule of thumb of *buy low and sell high!* Rebalancing can also be a good time to look for tax-loss harvesting opportunities. I personally believe in rebalancing, but the process of rebalancing is not a top priority for me, as it falls more into the category of an annual exercise. In fact, you should review your entire retirement plan annually to keep it current and on track to meet your goals.

All investment allocations recommended in this section assume the investor is in good health and is still working. If either personal health or loss of a job is a major threat, the allocations may be different. Remember, all investing has risks, and if your health history is a concern, more cash and shorter-term investments may make more sense than the broad age-based recommendations that follow.

A WORD OF CAUTION: Avoid making these common mistakes of beginning investors:

1. Waiting for the perfect time to invest. There is no such thing as the "perfect time to invest"! Research has shown that time in the market outperforms *timing* the market. A dollar invested at age 20 will produce a better payoff than one invested at age 25.

2. Trading frequently to capture small profits and losses. This is a day trader's strategy, and my rules of engagement encourage long-term investing rather than gambling on short-term trading. If you follow a day-trading approach, you will miss the advantages of a lower capital gains tax on investments held for a year or longer. Further, short-term trading is driven by emotion rather than stock valuations.

3. Picking a stock based on the latest news. This is a losing approach because you are already too late to get in on a stock before the market has gone higher. Individual investors are the last to hear this news, not the first.

4. Buying stocks because they are cheap. These stocks are typically penny stocks, with thinly traded volumes and limited information about the companies. Many of these companies are startups with higher risks. If you want

to buy pieces of quality companies with fewer dollars, I recommend using fractional-share purchases as a way to get started.

5. Cashing out of the market ("going to cash") because of bad economic news. The economic reality shows that most dips in the market have been short-lived and once you are out of the market, you run the risk of missing rebounding stock performance. I recommend a buy-and-hold strategy unless you absolutely need the funds to live on. Some consider "buying on the dips" to be a viable long-term strategy.

BETWEEN THE AGES OF 25–50 – At the age of 50 or younger, you are in the best position to take risks in your investment portfolio. If you make investment mistakes, there is time to correct them and make up any loss. This means growth is the focus of the majority of these investments. I personally believe that in this age range, investors should be 95% invested in common stocks with a 5% cash reserve. A broad index fund like Vanguard Total Stock Market Index Fund ETF Shares (VTI) is my fund of choice.

Stocks = VTI = 95%
Cash = 5% = money market funds

BETWEEN THE AGES OF 50–75 – Your time to recover from any investment mistakes has shortened, and your risk profile should reflect less risk. You still need growth-oriented investments, just not with as high an allocation. For stability and income, some bond funds could be a good choice. I like an allocation for this age range of 75% stocks, 20% bonds, and 5% cash.

Stocks = VTI = 75%
Bonds = 20% = split between BND and VTC
Cash = 5% = money market funds

I am a believer in the Vanguard Group of index funds/ETFs, as they have low expense ratios and a proven performance record over time. For bonds, I prefer the Vanguard Total Bond Market ETF (BND) and Vanguard Intermediate-Term Corporate Bond Fund (VTC). The most recent annualized expense ratios for each of them are shown below.

ANNUAL EXPENSE RATIO COMPARISON

- BND: 0.04%
- VTC: 0.05%
- VTI: 0.03%

Fixed-income investing remains a puzzle for most everyday investors while interest rates are low, sometimes nearing ZERO. There are some good opportunities in this asset category, and I have highlighted several of my favorites with the market symbols included in this chapter. There are similar bond index funds offered by Fidelity, Schwab, TD Ameritrade, and others, if you prefer other money managers.

OVER THE AGE OF 75 – From age 75 onward, I recommend a further reduction in your risk profile. This is the time to become more conservative in your investing philosophy. Growth is still needed to offer protection against inflation and the rising cost of living. The allocation percentage is less than the previous age category for stocks. My preferred allocation for this age range is 70% stocks, 25% bonds, and 5% cash.

Stocks = 70% = VTI
Bonds = 25% = split between BND and VTC
Cash = 5% = money market funds

The most conservative financial advisors recommend increasing the portion of your portfolio in fixed assets as you near or enter retirement. In fact, one of the most quoted advisors, John Bogle, recommends that the percentage of your portfolio in fixed income should equal your age. This is too conservative for me.

My reason for my continued recommendation of a 70% allocation to stock over the age of 75 is simple. At retirement, you already have a certain percentage of your assets in fixed-income securities: Social Security and/or an insurance annuity. This is in addition to the 25% I recommend in bonds.

Why maintain a minimum 5% cash reserve position in all three of these examples? Finding a balance between investments and cash reserves is always a challenge. History in the market has shown it pays to keep some cash on hand. A prudent investor should keep at least 5% of a portfolio in a cash reserve.

Cash can play multiple roles in a portfolio. Think of cash as dry powder—money available to take advantage of opportunities such as buying new investments at low costs, to lower the cost basis on existing investments, or to add a new income stream. Cash also provides a liquidity reserve if there is a time you can't turn other investments into cash for any reason.

Cash in a portfolio can also count as part of an investor's emergency fund. Aside from these realistic roles, cash can provide comfort to an investor as a psychological support that lends peace of mind. I always think of cash reserves in a portfolio as an anchor or source of comfort in case the financial markets become unhinged for any reason.

Investors often ask, "How long will one million dollars in savings last in retirement?" That depends on a number of things. The answer may partially depend on where you live in retirement. A recent study found that $1 million in savings was estimated to last 23 years in Mississippi compared with only 10 years in Hawaii.

WHERE YOU LIVE MAKES A DIFFERENCE[1]

STATE	ESTIMATED YEARS
Mississippi	23
Tennessee	22
Texas	21
Florida	20
Minnesota	19
Pennsylvania	18
Colorado	17
Massachusetts	15
New York	14
California	13
Hawaii	10

This analysis indicates the importance of deciding where you choose to maintain residency in retirement as a major factor in how long your savings can last. Where you live and the cost of living, other than housing, can have a major impact on your savings. Make this choice wisely, as the duration of your nest egg for financial support will depend on it.

Another consideration for many retirees is the question of relocating to a low-tax state. The tax difference among and between states is very clear. Florida, Texas, and Nevada have neither income nor estate taxes. New York and Connecticut have both. California doesn't have an estate tax, but its top personal

---

[1] The sources are the GOBankingRates analysis of Bureau of Labor Statistics data, in regard to expenditures; and the Missouri Economic Research and Information Center on cost of living.

income tax rate is the highest in the U.S. at 13.3%. The devil is always in the details, so be thorough in your research regarding any anticipated tax savings resulting from a relocation decision.

Finding a broadly diversified index fund or ETF is not difficult. Funds that track the S&P 500 index are broadly diversified, but even broader market exposure might track the total stock market or Wilshire 5000 or Russell 3000. Visit these websites for more information about index funds or ETFs:

1. www.NerdWallet.com
2. www.TheBalance.com
3. www.Fool.com
4. www.Wealthsimple.com
5. www.InvestmentTrends.com
6. www.Barrons.com

What about a draw-down (withdrawal rate) strategy during retirement? Many new retirees face the same conundrum: how best to draw down the assets in their retirement fund without running out of money? Various schools of thought are currently circulating on this topic:

- Spend only portfolio interest and dividends, and do not touch the principal.
- Withdraw 4% of the asset balance initially and adjust the dollar amount annually to keep pace with the cost of living.
- Base your annual spending on the required minimum distribution (RMD) rules that apply to traditional IRAs without an inflation adjustment.
- Spend taxable assets first, tax-deferred assets second, and tax-free assets last.
- Draw down lower-earning assets first and higher-earning assets last.

Finding a draw-down strategy that matches your individual needs and goals may require more than just a simple rule. There are tradeoffs with each of these strategies. Make sure you understand the tradeoffs of any strategy you choose.

My choice of draw-down strategies has been one that matches the mutual goals that my wife and I have set together. Our overall goals include maintaining a stable cash flow throughout retirement and leaving money to our heirs. Following a strategy based on the RMD rules has been the best approach to meet our goals. Since the RMD approach calculates the annual withdrawal as a percentage of the remaining portfolio balance annually, it is responsive to investment returns. This provides for an automatic, built-in inflation adjustment.

The annual RMD amount is calculated by dividing the year-end rollover IRA fund balance by a life expectancy factor for your age as listed in IRS Publication 590-B. The IRS RMD worksheets can also be found at www.IRS.gov by entering "IRS RMD calculator" as a search topic. Retirees of any age can use these resources as a spending guideline.

How does the 4% rule for withdrawals compare with the RMD withdrawal plan that follows the IRS guidelines? The 4% rule is close to the RMD approach but different. With the 4% rule, retirees are withdrawing a static number adjusted for inflation. As the retirement fund balance shrinks, the static number becomes unsustainable, as it can quickly exceed the initial 4% calculation. The risk of running out of money increases.

Using the RMD approach is different because the annual withdrawal amount is based on the previous year-end retirement account balance and, therefore, the risk of running out of money is eliminated. This is another reason my wife and I prefer the

RMD approach as the withdrawal strategy that works best for us. You need to find the draw-down strategy that best matches your personal goals.

Just a cautionary note: No draw-down strategy is perfect. In a projected extended period of low interest rates and lower expected returns, I am more comfortable with keeping spending rates more conservative. There is no simple rule for spending retirement assets that matches every retiree's needs. Be careful with your choice of a draw-down strategy.

Sometimes readers prefer to see an example of investment selections rather than just words. Here is an example of building a diversified investment account over time.

ASSUMPTIONS

- This is ONE taxable account with multiple investment options.
- These examples follow the age-based recommendations outlined earlier in this chapter; any IRAs or 401(k) balances are NOT included.
- From age 25 to 75, $500 is invested per month. Monthly contributions are made through automatic transfers from the checking to the investment account.
- A steady yield of 5% accrues annually.
- No withdrawals are made over the entire timespan.

BALANCE AT AGE 50 (25 YEARS)

VTI @ 95% = $280,915
CASH @ 5% = 14,785
TOTAL = $295,700

BALANCE AT AGE 75 (25 YEARS)

VTI @ 75% = $971,625
BND @ 10% = 129,550
VTC @ 10% = 129,550
CASH @ 5% = 64,775

TOTAL = $1,295,500

FUNDS AVAILABLE AT AGE 75 FOR ENJOYING RETIREMENT

VTI @ 70% = $910,000
BND @ 13% = 169,000
VTC @ 12% = 156,000
CASH @ 5% = 65,000

TOTAL = $1,300,000 (rounded up)

There you have it. I have presented my thoughts on building an investment portfolio with age-related risk mitigation. If you are looking for the maximum benefit of diversification, choosing among the index funds and ETFs contained within the websites listed in this chapter will meet your need for a broad-based investment fund. I have also discussed how to build a comfortable, complete retirement fund and the need to use caution in selecting a draw-down strategy that matches your goals. Be very careful not to follow any one draw-down strategy blindly, as your need for money will change over time. Maintaining financial flexibility is one of the advantages of having a well-funded retirement plan.

CHAPTER FOURTEEN

FOCUS ON LIVING

Let's face it, we all would like to live the good life in retirement. The definition of "the good life" will be different for each of us, but at a minimum, we want to live a fulfilling retirement.

Thanks to a growing list of options, deciding where to live in retirement can be a challenge—but also part of "living the good life." If you have always dreamed of living near the ocean, retirement is a great time to take action and make that happen. The same holds true if you have always wanted to live in the mountains or in the desert, or to just spend more time in a warmer climate. Retirement can be a great time to make those dreams a reality.

The common thread among any relocation aspiration is the question of affordability. Can you afford to relocate? This is one of the benefits of having saved and invested most of your adult life in building a retirement nest egg. Relocation is always more expensive than anticipated, but it can be very satisfying in your golden years. With a well-funded retirement account, the answer to the relocation question can be, *YES!*

For many, just establishing a new routine in retirement, maintaining social connections, staying healthy, and continuing to learn new things can be very rewarding. Maintaining family connections also plays a major role in defining "living a good life."

Whatever your definition of "a good life," make it happen and enjoy your retired lifestyle.

At the same time, do not be afraid of continuing to experience change in retirement. Managing change has always been a part of life, and the pace of change seems to quicken in retirement. Changes in routine and other unplanned events sometimes add stress to one's retirement years, but having a flexible mindset will help. Make an effort to maintain an active lifestyle and avoid social isolation and withdrawal. These symptoms can lead to serious mental and physical health issues.

Life expectancy is increasing, so more Americans will have the potential to enjoy more years in retirement. Some researchers have speculated that retirement could last 40 years for some, which is more than their time spent working. At some point, quality of life may also become an issue.

Some retirees say they are considerably less concerned than pre-retirees about their money lasting throughout retirement, but they worry more about the financial and lifestyle implications of declining health, according to new research from Massachusetts Mutual Life Insurance Co. (MassMutual).

"While many retirees can manage their expenses to lower income levels in retirement, the rising cost of care may steadily reduce their lifestyles as they age," says Tom Foster, Jr., Head of Retirement Plans Practice Management with MassMutual. "Once you're older, it may be impossible to make up for any increasing income needs by simply tightening your belt. It's far better to err on the side of having more rather than less income than you anticipate needing, especially as costs for care continue to escalate."

In real life, not all retirements are the result of your personal choice. How should you proceed if the pandemic or another economic or health situation or mandatory retirement age has forced your departure from the workforce before you've reached the age to qualify for full retirement benefits?

If you are retiring ahead of schedule for reasons beyond your control, you need to focus on obtaining continuing healthcare coverage and closing the savings gap you may have by being asked to retire earlier than planned. Consider taking these actions quickly, if you are surprised by an unplanned retirement:

- Decrease spending quickly. Take action to conserve your monthly cash flow by cutting back on all unnecessary expenses, cutting the cord to cable TV and a landline and avoiding all big expenditures.
- Maintain health coverage through COBRA. This will give you time to explore the market for less expensive coverage. COBRA allows you to stay in your employer's plan for up to 18 months after you leave their employment, as long as you pay the premiums directly. Maintaining health insurance coverage until Medicare eligibility at age 65 is vital.
- You may need to access your retirement savings early. Check with a financial advisor to determine the best way to do this without penalties or taxes.
- Continue to protect your Social Security benefits. Do NOT rush to file for these benefits. The longer you can wait (up to age 70) before you start benefits, the larger your monthly check will be for the rest of your life. Unless you absolutely need those monthly payments to live, defer for as long as you can.

So much has changed in the world of finance since you began your career. When it comes to what to do with your money, you have many new options. So, what should you do? What options are best for you?

I recommend you choose almost none of them! Rather, I prefer the advice of financial writer Jane Bryant Quinn: "Simplify your financial life. Raise the automatic contribution to your savings plans. Automate contributions to an individual retirement account (IRA). Buy low-cost index funds that follow the broad stock and bond markets, as they will likely outperform any managed fund you own or any bag of individual stocks you might select. Right-size your life to live within your means. Make a will. Check that the beneficiary forms of your IRA and 401(k)s list the correct people. Then quit thinking about your money and get on with your life. Simple is the sophisticated way to save, invest and plan."

In a few words, *keep it simple!*

There's a lot of life to live between now and when you retire, so focusing exclusively on financial planning for retirement could be a mistake. There are many other shorter-term goals and milestones in life that you want to enjoy, like time spent with a growing family, buying a home, traveling, or pursuing a different career. Don't sacrifice so much today that you feel deprived and miss out on the experiences that memories are made from. Balancing all of these priorities is difficult but necessary. Retirement is a time when you come face to face with the significance of the choices you have made in the past.

Hopefully the retirement you envision includes more than sleeping late every day, making your doctor's appointments, and visiting family on holidays. While this may sound like what you want to do in retirement, such a life will become boring pretty quickly. It is important to have something else to do other than "not go to work." All of us need a sense of purpose.

The National Institute on Aging (NIA) says that taking part in meaningful activities can keep your brain active and help you feel happier, healthier, and less isolated. Balancing life in retirement is all about maintaining a sense of purpose.

Purpose may involve assisting other family members who count on you, volunteering for your favorite charity, working part-time, maintaining an established schedule providing respite relief care for a friend, or just spending time visiting and delivering food to the elderly or disabled.

When you awaken each day in retirement, it will feel comforting to know you have a purpose to fulfill that day and everyday. With purpose comes a sense of serenity with fewer worries, more frequent socialization, and a greater mission to accomplish.

When you think about your life up to the present, the two things that probably matter the most are the experiences you've had and the people with whom you shared them. Keep your life rich by continuing to enjoy new experiences. Life is woven from infinite possibilities.

I hope you will remain curious about life. With so many resources available, such as online news available 24/7, documentaries, learning resources like Ancestry.com, the books of great writers, and many others, it should be easy to find topics to stimulate your curiosity. Accumulating knowledge never gets old.

Enjoy nature, too, as it is all around you and it is not expensive. As you go through your daily life, appreciate the natural beauty around you. A brilliant sunrise, the blooming flowers and trees, the birds, the quietness of your backyard, the sky, clouds, and a warm breeze and a beautiful sunset should never be taken for granted. There is no promise of tomorrow.

Along with living life every day and planning for retirement, set some lifestyle goals. These goals should reflect what you want your life to be like in the future. Ask yourself these questions for each potential goal you have in mind: "Is it possible?" "Who will I share it with?" and "What do I need to do now and in the near-term to complete these goals?" Following this approach could lead you to a happier and more fulfilling retirement lifestyle. Retirement is what you make of it.

My point all along is that there is no "right" or "best" retirement. There is only **your** retirement, one that follows a plan designed and implemented with your spouse. The planning process will improve your chances of having a more fulfilling retirement.

Focus on *living*! Don't let the past drag you down, and don't let the future frighten you. Feel good in the *now*, for the important time is the present. Life is full of uncertainties, but one sure fact remains: retirement financial security is within your reach. Make retirement planning your priority!

CONCLUSION

"Success is not the key to happiness.
Happiness is the key to success."
– Albert Schweitzer –

How long will you live? How long does your money need to last?
It's impossible to answer these two questions. We only have a sense
of how long people live on average. The number that matters most
is how long **you** will live.

Personal economic security has always been a major issue in an
unstable, sometimes unequal world with an aging population.
This worry about personal financial security has prompted many
different retirement planning ideas and proposals. The move
away from corporate-sponsored pension plans was an intentional
effort to transfer responsibility for retirement funding and
administration away from the employer directly to the employee.

The current looming retirement crisis facing Americans is self-
made. It is not the result of a government conspiracy or the fault
of any political party or your employer. Your financial future
depends on what you actually do, not on what you *want* to do.
The reasons for many underfunded retirement accounts are self-
inflicted. It is YOUR FAULT!

I know this may sound harsh, but sometimes the truth hurts. Call
it tough love. Over the past few decades, retirement planning has
shifted to become each individual's responsibility. Blame no one

else if your retirement fund is less than you had hoped to have by the time you give up your regular paycheck.

Hope springs eternal, and so do our best wishes for a secure retirement. It is not too late to change the direction of your retirement funding to improve your outcomes. Reading this book is a good start, but it will take more than crossing this title off your reading list. It will take *action* on your part.

For one thing, the looming retirement crisis can be improved upon or completely avoided. Everyday investors can save more and demonstrate financial discipline, if they choose to. The truth is, most of us don't really need all of the "stuff" we acquire during our working years. Building a retirement nest egg would be a better use of our funds.

Public employees are one cohort that still enjoys having access to a pension program. But many of these public pension plans find themselves underfunded, and concern has increased about being able to meet all of their pension liabilities. It seems the pending retirement crisis has crept into corners of the public sector as well.

Some retired city workers are feeling squeezed on their healthcare. New Jersey, Michigan, Connecticut, Kentucky, and Texas have reduced healthcare benefits, tightened eligibility requirements, or increased premiums, according to the National Association of State Retirement Administrators. Most state governments have legal protections for their workers' pension plans, but not all have protections for retiree health plans.

Few things can cause people to protest and riot in the streets faster than the threat of cuts to pensions and entitlements like Social Security and Medicare. We have not seen these protests in the

U.S. as of yet, but France, Greece, Italy, and Chile are examples of where this has recently happened. People everywhere worry they won't have enough money to retire. Retirement security is a universal concern.

I have discussed a number of investment strategies throughout this book. Now, let's take a look at a summary of the basic investments I have recommended. What level of retirement fund balance would you have, if these examples performed as discussed? All illustrations assume investing begins at age 30.

- Investing $500 per month in an IRA earning a consistent annual return of 5.0% would produce a balance after 30 years of $411,500; after 35 years, $559,200; and after 40 years, $747,800. (Annual contributions are limited to $6,000.)
- Investing $1,625 per month in an employer-sponsored 401(k) plan without any company matches, earning a consistent 5.0% return, would produce a balance after 30 years of $1,337,400; after 35 years, $1,817,500; and after 40 years, $2,430,300. (Annual contributions are limited to $19,500.)
- Investing $500 per month in a stock index fund earning a consistent 5.0% return would produce a balance after 30 years of $411,500; after 35 years, $559,200; and after 40 years, $747,800.

These results do not reflect any potential tax advantages an investor might receive as a result of qualifying IRA deductions and income tax reductions from 401(k) contributions.

SUMMARY OF RETIREMENT FUND BALANCES

Type of Investment	30 years	35 years	40 years
IRA	411,500	559,200	747,800
401(k)	1,337,400	1,817,500	2,430,300
Additional Investments	411,500	559,200	747,800
TOTAL	$2,160,400	$2,935,900	$3,925,900

Here is how all of this comes together in these examples. IRA investments are limited to $6,000 per year; 401(k) investments are limited to $19,500 per year; and the additional $500 per month investment totals $6,000 per year. None of these annual amounts were changed over the 40-year life of these examples.

TOTAL INVESTED CAPITAL

Type of investment	30 years	35 years	40 years
IRA	180,000	210,000	240,000
401(k)	585,000	682,500	780,000
Additional Investment	180,000	210,000	240,000
TOTAL	$945,000	$1,102,500	$1,260,000

Saving—early, often, and regularly—is the key to wealth building. It's as simple as that! But it is also mission critical. Individuals must find a way to crack the code of saving while also pursuing a career and enjoying life. Those who do crack the code will discover that it will yield major rewards in the future.

The 30-year comparison of projected investment results with the total invested capital reveals a net gain of $1,215,400. The longer money is invested, the greater the potential positive contribution to your retirement funds. This is good retirement planning in action.

Projected investment results:	$2,160,400
Total invested capital:	945,000
Net positive gain:	$1,215,400

Studies have documented the savings gap appearing on many Americans' financial statements. I have shared strategies to improve your savings accumulations by investing for the long-term rather than speculating, postponing taking the first payments from Social Security for as long as you can (until age 70), and always managing investment costs to lower expenses. Lower costs win over time.

Most of the discussion in this book has centered on the importance of saving for retirement. While the topic of saving is important, so is your plan of action for investing when you enter retirement. Once you have successfully navigated the accumulation phase, it is critical to put into motion how you will convert those assets to income.

There are many options that can play an integral role in your retirement planning. I have highlighted a few, but I encourage you to talk with a financial advisor to review more options and select the ones that may be most relevant to your circumstances.

Remember, successful retirement planning does not occur in isolation. It is ongoing as you pursue a career, raise a family, and deal with all that life has to offer. There is no good retirement solution without tradeoffs. Striving to do all of the following will help ensure you reach your financial goals for retirement.

- Making life choices that increase your savings and funds for investment.
- Living within your means and keeping debt low and manageable.
- Building an emergency or contingency fund for unforeseen expenses.
- Foregoing short-term consumption to provide for long-term benefits.
- Understanding that making tradeoffs can provide for more saving early, often, and regularly.
- Aiming to save 15% of pre-tax income as a goal and automating the process.

Having access to multiple sources of income in retirement will result from these tradeoffs. Living a purposeful life in retirement while making the most of each day is the ultimate benefit of having made these choices.

I also want to acknowledge that throughout this book, discussion swings between a personal pension plan and a retirement plan. It is important to distinguish between the two. A personal pension plan is ONE COMPONENT of an overall retirement plan. A retirement plan has multiple other components in addition to a personal pension plan. The graphic in Chapter Twelve best illustrates the interconnectedness of these components.

Here are the most important things I wanted readers to take away from *PATHWAY TO A PENSION*:

1. Saving and investing for retirement is *your* responsibility.
2. Many Boomers turning age 65 are unprepared for retirement. If you are not a Boomer, will you continue to follow them over the edge, or will you correct course?

3. When you reach retirement age, it is too late for a financial do-over.

4. To do nothing is a choice! You will either suffer the consequences of this choice or enjoy the benefits of choosing retirement planning that will allow you to meet your retirement timeline.

5. Retirement planning is NOT for "old people." It's what successful people do. Be intentional, focusing on reaching your retirement goals. It's never too early to start planning for your future.

6. Retiring with the security blanket provided by a personal pension is possible. With planning, you can build a pension plan and put your retirement insecurity to rest with your own check-a-month plan.

7. Americans lack adequate financial literacy and retirement planning education. It is time to educate yourself in both areas.

8. Healthcare and long-term care for seniors faces growing challenges as the number of people over the age of 65 increases. Incorporate these rising cost estimates in your retirement plans.
   Consider funding an HSA account to address medical expenses in retirement.

9. Low interest rates may help the economy recover and thrive, but they can be harmful to seniors living on a fixed income. Anticipate a period of low interest rates and lower returns over the next five years.

10. My Rules of Engagement can help you achieve the financial retirement you want. It can be your time to enjoy the things you have always wanted to do.

11. *PATHWAY TO A PENSION* gives everyday investors a way to move ahead, breaking the logjam caused by inertia, to secure a lifetime retirement paycheck.

If you feel uncomfortable being a DIY investor, engage a financial advisor to guide you toward achieving your retirement goals. Successful retirement is more than just enjoying financial independence. It's also about finding meaning and purpose in your life. You can learn how to maximize your financial resources to fund this quest.

Why not unravel the mysteries of building a personal pension plan by taking a few measured steps early in your career and letting time be your best friend? If you miss this opportunity early in life, it is not too late to fund a retirement nest egg, however. Just don't wait too long.

The time-honored solution for a crisis or a panic attack is actionable information. **PATHWAY TO A PENSION** is overflowing with actionable advice. Put it to work for you and your family.

Retirement should be the golden years of your life. After a lifetime of work and saving, you deserve to live a golden retirement, including the benefits of good health, having enough money, and enjoying all that goes with "living the good life." Don't settle for anything less! There is no expiration date for retirement planning. It just becomes a plan with fewer options when time is no longer your friend. Time has become very finite once you reach full retirement age (FRA).

I hope this book has been engaging and has offered some inspiration to help you build a personal pension plan, as part of a more comprehensive retirement plan. A well-funded retirement portfolio can give you the peace of mind that will allow you to focus on other things like pursuing a more productive and meaningful life in retirement.

I started this book with several common themes in mind: a looming retirement crisis; a need to save early, often, and regularly;

and the need to develop a retirement plan. Following these themes led to my SIMPLE PENSION PLAN, which can be augmented to become a more ROBUST PENSION PLAN if needed. We have also covered investment strategies and the need for age-mitigated investment combinations. After this, the rest is up to you.

There are different paths leading to the creation of a personal pension plan. *PATHWAY TO A PENSION* is one of them. Find a path that works best for your specific circumstances and follow it to a secure and financially rewarding retirement.

Facts are necessary things whether you are launching a rocket into space, picking a stock or other investment, or writing a nonfiction book like *PATHWAY TO A PENSION*. I have made every effort to ensure the facts presented are accurate and relevant to the subject matter. I consider earning your trust on this subject to be a personal goal and a valued achievement.

CONGRATULATIONS, if you have reached this point in the book! You've refined your understanding of the need for saving, investing, managing costs, and investing for the long-term. You have reviewed my seven Rules of Engagement. When you put them into action, you'll be well on your way to securing a lifetime retirement paycheck. Together, let's rewrite the story of your retirement.

I wish you the best on your journey to an amazing new chapter in life as you transition toward retirement. Make it the best it can be! Saving early, often, and regularly is the gravitational center of retirement planning. Take charge of YOUR retirement. If you can save, you will be on a journey leading to a fulfilling retirement while following *PATHWAY TO A PENSION*.

A final note about this most unusual and uncertain past year. As you know, 2020 was the year the world turned upside down. It was a challenging year unlike any other in our lifetimes, with the majority of Americans suffering from a massive dose of pandemic fatigue. It tested our patience, resolve, and fortitude to "keep on keepin' on," as Bob Dylan has phrased it in a song. As a nation, we have endured a lost sense of purpose for most of the past year.

Overall, 2020 was not a normal year. It was a year most of us want to forget, with the surging pandemic, entire community lockdowns, a shortage of toilet paper and baking ingredients, economic stress, death, and illness. High unemployment, loan deferments, rent relief, and suspended evictions for nonpayment are but a few of the holdovers to be dealt with in 2021.

It has been a year of fear, but we can finally exhale and optimistically await the availability of the COVID-19 vaccines that are being distributed. These vaccines are so welcome and needed, representing a giant leap forward that will allow for a return to a familiar rhythm of life for all of us. This is how we return to a more "normal" lifestyle.

Throughout this nation, we have a newly discovered gratitude for the people who work on the front lines of our economy, who keep the country functioning. These are our real heroes. This gratitude extends to grocery store employees, truckers, farmers, police and fire departments, hospitals, nurses, doctors, healthcare workers of all categories, laboratory researchers, and the custodial staffs that keep these organizations clean and open for business. There are too many heroes who deserve our personal thanks to mention.

Throughout this pandemic, we have learned what Americans are made of and how resilient we truly are. We have traveled through this together, and we are stronger as a result.

I have seen a lot during my lifetime, and I know we are going to recover when this pandemic is over. Let's put the pandemic of 2020 in the rearview mirror but continue to embrace our real heroes going forward.

I appreciate every reader and your continued support. I look forward to having the opportunity for in-person book-signing events soon! We all eagerly anticipate what 2021 has in store. I hope that for you, it is a rewarding year filled with opportunities to reach your goals while fully enjoying the present.

ACKNOWLEDGEMENTS

I wish to thank my wife for her unwavering patience during the research and writing process. My wife has always been a contributing member of our publishing team. She has cautioned me numerous times to keep my hand on the wheel and my eyes on the road whenever I have wanted to steer in a different direction. Helping me stay focused and on topic is one of her many admirable qualities. I am forever grateful for her guidance and wise counsel.

To family members and friends who have been supportive throughout the years, I owe my appreciation to all of you. You have been exactly the up-close and personal allies I needed during these uncertain times.

It really does take the support of a village to complete a book. There are too many daily distractions and interruptions to record. To all who have inspired me to stay on topic and write on this subject in so many different ways, I offer my sincere appreciation for your encouragement.

I hope *PATHWAY TO A PENSION* offers constructive guidance to anyone seeking a more secure retirement. Achieving a lifetime retirement paycheck is a realistic opportunity for you.

RESOURCES

I. Articles in Periodicals and Research Papers

    1. National Association of State Retirement Administrators Survey
    2. GOBankingRates Survey
    3. National Institutes on Aging Study
    4. National Institute on Retirement Security Study
    5. MassMutual Retirement Survey
    6. 2019 Retirement Confidence Survey
    7. *The Wall Street Journal*
    8. *Workforce Crisis*, published by Harvard Business School Press
    9. Oxford English Dictionary

II. Websites

    1. www.AARP.org
    2. www.TheBalance.com
    3. www.Bankrate.com
    4. www.Barrons.com
    5. www.Fool.com
    6. www.InvestmentTrends.com
    7. www.IRS.gov
    8. www.NerdWallet.com
    9. www.OpportunityCost.com
    10. www.PewResearch.org
    11. www.Prosper.com
    12. www.SSA.gov
    13. www.Wealthsimple.com

III. Quotations

1. John Carswell, historian
2. Ken Dychtwald, entrepreneur and author
3. President Dwight D. Eisenhower
4. Tom Foster, Jr., MassMutual
5. Sander Levin
6. Jane Bryant Quinn, financial journalist
7. John D. Rockefeller
8. Albert Schweitzer, theologian
9. Antoine de Saint-Exupéry, French author
10. Andy Smith, radio host